COUNTRY
FAIR
FOOD & CRAFTS

This edition published in 1994 by SMITHMARK
Publishers Inc., 16 East 32nd Street, New York, NY
10016

SMITHMARK books are available for bulk purchase
for sales promotion and premium use. For details
write or call the manager of special sales,
SMITHMARK Publishers Inc., 16 East 32nd Street,
New York, NY 10016; (212) 532-6600

Food Editors: Rachel Blackmore, Sheryle Eastwood
Craft Editors: Judy Poulos, Tonia Todman
Subeditor: Sheridan Packer
Assistant Craft Editor: Sally Pereira
Editorial Assistant: Marian Broderick
Editorial Coordinator: Margaret Kelly
Text: Vicky Fraser, Denise Greig, Judy Poulos
Craft Assistance: Kate Fury, Elsie Hamerlok,
Sophie Levitt, Sue Leech, Louise Pfanner, Cecily
Rogers, Carol Todman

Photography: Andrew Elton
Styling: Michelle Gorry

Production Managers: Sheridan Carter, Anna
Maguire
Layout and Design: Lulu Dougherty, Monica
Kessler-Tay
Finished Art: Chris Hatcher
Cover Design: Frank Pithers

Some of the contents of this book have been
previously published in other J.B. Fairfax Press
publications.

JBFP 325 US
Country Fair Food & Crafts
Includes Index
ISBN 0 8317 1228 7

Produced by J.B. Fairfax Press Pty Limited
Printed by Toppan Printing Co, Singapore
PRINTED IN SINGAPORE
10 9 8 7 6 5 4 3 2 1

COUNTRY
FAIR
FOOD & CRAFTS

SMITHMARK

CHECK-AND-SHOP

When planning to bake goodies or create a selection of craft items for your market stall or local bazaar, use the easy Check-and-Shop boxes which appear beside all the recipe ingredients and craft materials. Simply look on your pantry shelf or in your sewing kit and if what you need isn't there, check the boxes as a reminder to add those items to your shopping list.

SAFETY NOTE

If you are making stuffed toys for your sale, use saftey eyes and noses or glued-on felt facial features. Buttons, bows and other loose trimmings should not be used if toys are for babies or very small children.

Contents

How to plan for profit　　　　6

Cake delights　　　　10

Sweet temptations　　　　26

Gourmet delicacies　　　　36

Take-along treats　　　　42

Garden crafts　　　　46

Packaging & presentation　　　　52

Craft creations　　　　54

Gift treasures　　　　72

Christmas corner　　　　86

Index　　　　94

Introduction

Country fairs and charity bazaars go back a long way.
For centuries such festivities have brought us together to celebrate fine
food, crafts, lively entertainment and great bargains. Today's fairs and
markets still have that wonderful sense of excitement and, whether
they are cosy get-togethers at the local school, the annual church
bazaar or full-scale extravangazas, they usually offer a fantastic
selection of beautiful handicrafts and delicious homemade sweets and
"savories". These days, fairs and bazaars are not only festive and fun
occasions but also major fundraising events.
Perhaps this year it's your turn to go behind the scenes and make it all
happen. Don't worry! Organising a fair or bazaar can be lots of fun,
and very rewarding. What better way is there to raise much-needed
funds for your school or church group?
In this book, you'll find great ideas and helpful advice
to make your next fair a roaring success.

How to plan for profit

Organizing a fundraising fair or bazaar takes time – from three months to a year. The real key to success is an active and energetic planning committee who can inspire others to participate in preparing and running the fair.

Each booth should have its own committee, made up of a chairperson, secretary and treasurer and as many members as needed to make a comfortable working group. The committee is responsible for making or collecting the goods for sale, seeking donations of raw materials or prizes and setting up and running the booth on the day of the fair. To raise money for operating expenses, the committee might run fundraising social events prior to the fair. The money raised can be used to buy raw ingredients, packaging materials, and whatever is needed to construct and decorate the booth.

It is essential for each booth to have a team of reliable, eager volunteers. Enlist the help of as many people as you can, especially those with the special talents you require for your booth. Welcome all volunteers; everyone will contribute something to the preparations.

Let each person determine how much work they are willing to do. If the items to be sold must be made, try to supply your helpers with some or all of the raw materials they will need for the job.

Meetings will be necessary, but they need not be boring, dragged-out affairs. If it is run in a relaxed, informal way, a meeting can be lots of fun and a great way to get people involved and busy.

Regular meetings are important for planning, assigning tasks and reviewing progress. They also provide great opportunities for sharing ideas and skills. The committee secretaries should take careful notes.

THE COUNTDOWN

With so many tasks to be completed over several months, a countdown calendar is an excellent way to track your progress. Tracking is especially important for craft items and other goods that are time-consuming to make or may need to mature, such as plants and relishes. To make a countdown calendar:

❖ Start with the "big" date and work backwards, plotting the completion dates for each stage of preparation.

Left: Fancy items make great raffle prizes

Right: Good presentation is a must

- Be a little flexible, allowing extra time for the unexpected. Things rarely go exactly as planned.
- Review your calendar regularly and, if necessary, reassess the dates.

As with all successful ventures, effective organization will help you anticipate problems and minimize frustration.

MONEY, MONEY, MONEY!

To run a successful fair, you must take a fairly professional approach toward money matters, including fund-raising, budgeting and setting targets, and handling money on the day of the fair. The planning committee should follow these simple guidelines:

- Determine how much money you want to raise. Set a target based on last year's earnings, plus a modest increase.
- Estimate the total costs involved in producing the goods and setting up the booths.
- To minimize expenses, try to have raw materials donated or purchase them at a discount rate.
- Don't overlook hidden costs, such as insurance, security, hall or equipment rental and trash collection.
- You may wish to allow customers to pay for their purchases with credit cards – if so, your bank can help you establish a merchant credit card system. Rates vary, so plan ahead and shop around.
- You will need a secure area for holding and counting money on the day of the fair. Ideally it will be a room, large enough for three or four people, with a single access which is easily locked.

If your fair is being run to benefit a nonprofit or charitable organization, you may be exempt from paying or collecting sales tax. Rules vary from state to state. Contact your state department of revenue or taxation for information.

Pricing is always a thorny problem – generally, buyers are looking for bargains, but will be happy to pay a little more for something truly special and desirable.

Take into account how much an item costs to make when deciding on price. Remember that you may have to discount perishable items toward the end of the day. Generally prices should be a little below the local retail prices for similar items, but always allow a premium for something handmade and unique.

Before opening for business, make sure each booth has a reasonable amount of change to start with. Don't allow large amounts of money to be kept at the booth – arrange for two reliable people to collect money from each booth at regular intervals. Hold all collected money in your secure room until it can be counted and banked.

PUBLICITY

The more publicity you generate beforehand, the better attended your fair will be. Appoint a publicity officer to plan a well-organized campaign using a variety of methods to attract attention to the event.

Look for opportunities for free publicity – public service announcements on community cable TV and radio stations, and diary dates in local newspapers are good starting points. If you have a particularly newsworthy attraction at the fair or a celebrity to open it, contact the features editor of the newspaper with details.

Local merchants are usually willing to place notices or posters for worthy causes in their windows. Some may even be prepared to hand out leaflets to customers. Why not organize a competition among local youngsters to design a fair poster? There should be a prize for the winner, and all the posters – winners and losers alike – should be exhibited. Remind parents of a school fair by sending notices home with the children. Large banners (the larger the better) and colored bunting are great attention-getters, so make sure they are strategically placed around the fair site at least two weeks beforehand.

If you can afford paid publicity, it may be worthwhile to invest in advertising in the local press or printing and delivering leaflets around the neighborhood.

PLANNING THE EVENT

Planning a fundraising event usually begins with setting a date. Choose a day that does not clash with public holidays or other local events. If you need to select and book a hall, do so as early as possible and ask for confirmation in writing.

When planning booths, include the traditional attractions such as the cake, cookies and candies, gourmet foods and craft booths. These are great money-makers and, together with a range of entertainment to suit all ages, will provide a good nucleus. In the pages to follow, you'll find wonderful ideas for booths and lots of hints on how to run them.

Make sure you provide plenty of tempting refreshments – hamburgers and hotdogs, sandwiches, muffins, even candy apples. A popcorn or cotton candy machine (rent one from a party rental center) is a great draw for the refreshment stand. And don't forget the ice! Rent an ice maker for the day, or buy ice cubes in bulk and store them in ice chests

or a freezer. Provide a quiet, comfortable retreat for harassed parents, friends and organizers to sit down for a soda or cup of coffee.

Raffles and door prizes are excellent attractions. Announce winners during the course of the day. Some booths can organize their own raffles. Plan these well in advance and check with state or town authorities about regulations governing raffles or prize drawings. Ask local businesses for prizes and have offers confirmed in writing. Ask a local celebrity to present the prizes.

TIMETABLE OF EVENTS

When planning the program for the day, remember there will be lots of cleaning and packing up to do after closing time and everyone will be tired. Since lunchtime is the busiest part of the day, schedule one major event before midday and another in the early afternoon.

Appoint a master of ceremonies to announce events over a public address system. If booths have their own loudspeakers, make sure they don't compete with each other. Have volunteers dressed as clowns

Scented sachets filled with lavender and potpourri

or minstrels wandering through the crowd and spreading the word about attractions.

DESIGNING A FLOOR PLAN

When deciding where to position the booths, consider which ones require electrical outlets, water taps or shady locations (for outdoor fairs).

Include an area for first aid, lost children and lost property, and indicate the location of rest rooms clearly. If you provide parking, set aside an area close to the booths for volunteer workers so they don't have too far to carry their goods. If your fair covers a large area, post signs to direct people to stands and activities.

If you're planning an outdoor fair, your greatest fear probably is waking up on the big day to an overcast sky and the threat of rain. Always have a back-up plan in case of wet weather and make sure everyone is aware of the alternative arrangements. Without advance planning all your efforts could be washed down the drain!

BOOTH DECORATION

A friendly, appealing booth attracts customers. Be as imaginative and creative as you like – it will certainly pay off with sales. Use a theme, such as the "gay 90s", to unite the various booths and activities.

Cover stands with fabric or paper and use shelving, baskets and the support poles of the stand to display your wares. Balloons and streamers are excellent and inexpensive ways to create a festive atmosphere. Color and fun should be the order of the day!

Packaging is equally important. Make goods irresistible by using lots of cellophane paper, pretty ribbon and decorative price tags.

If you are looking for inspiration, the wealth of creative ideas for presentation, packaging and displays you'll find in this book are guaranteed to set you on the right path.

ON THE DAY

Depending on security and the type of booth, you may be able to set up and at least partially stock some stands the night before. If not, allow plenty of time before the opening and recruit volunteers to help set up and decorate each booth. Don't clutter the display – keep extra stock in boxes under the counter or in a cool place and replenish the booth regularly from these reserves.

Create a duty roster for those manning the booths so that everyone has some time off to enjoy the event. Lunchtime is likely to be one of the busiest times, especially if you are selling food, so schedule extra people during this time. You will also need a team of willing helpers to clean up and dismantle everything at closing time. Arrange with your town sanitation service for trash removal at the end of the day's festivities.

Activity, like an open barbecue, makes the refreshment stand exciting

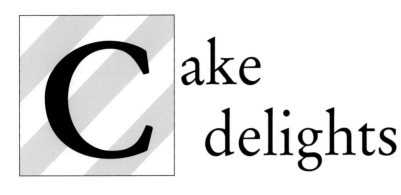

Cake delights

The cake booth, with its wonderful array of goodies, is always popular and profitable. Few people can resist the temptation of a beautifully presented selection of home-baked cakes and cookies.

A wide range of high quality cakes and cookies is the key to a successful booth. Sell some cakes by-the-slice for folks to munch as they browse.

Divide your baking between cakes and cookies, and draw up a master plan for each. The plan should cover:

- basic recipes
- cooking, storing and packaging instructions
- completion date, collection point and special transportation instructions
- flavor and icing variations, the size or shape of the cake pan required, and tips on cake baking and icing

Give each "baker" a master plan, with assigned recipes and variations indicated, together with the quantities she or he has agreed to make.

Most baked goods can be made then frozen without icing. If you ice cakes while they are still frozen the icing will set faster.

Arrange to have all your baked goods delivered to a central point for packaging the day before.

Wrap cookies in decorative tins, boxes covered in fabric or small cellophane bags attractively tied with curling ribbon.

To wrap cakes, cut a circle of strong cardboard 3/4 inch larger all around than the cake. Place the cardboard on a circle of cellophane about twice the diameter of the cardboard. Cover the cardboard with a doily and place the cake on it. Taking care not to touch the icing, gather up the cellophane over the cake and tie with ribbon. Use cake boxes for larger cakes which may be difficult to wrap.

PRICES

Keep prices below local retail prices. The lower the cost of ingredients, the higher your profits will be. If ingredients aren't donated, buy them in bulk from a wholesaler. Price each item clearly.

DECORATION

Decorating the booth can be lots of fun. Keep the feeling light and airy – like your cakes! If you can, incorporate shelving into the booth (painted bricks and wooden planks are inexpensive and effective) to give your display height and depth. Use baskets to hold cookies packed in cellophane bags or stack boxed biscuits around the booth. Keep a variety of cakes and slices on display at all times. Keep a supply of cakes in a cool place to replenish your stock during the day.

❖

BEST EVER CHOCOLATE CAKE

Makes 10 servings

- ☐ $^3/_4$ **cup unsweetened cocoa powder**
- ☐ $1^1/_2$ **cups boiling water**
- ☐ $^3/_4$ **cup butter or margarine**
- ☐ $1^3/_4$ **cup sugar**
- ☐ **2 tablespoons raspberry jam**
- ☐ **3 eggs**
- ☐ $2^1/_2$ **cups self-rising flour, sifted**

FROSTING
- ☐ $^1/_2$ **cup (1 stick) butter or margarine (softened)**
- ☐ **2 cups IOX (confectioners') sugar, sifted**
- ☐ $1^1/_2$ **tablespoons unsweetened cocoa powder, sifted**
- ☐ **2 teaspoons instant coffee powder**
- ☐ **2 tablespoons milk**

DECORATION
- ☐ **Glacé cherries (optional)**
- ☐ **Silver dragées (optional)**

1 Preheat the oven to moderate (350°). Grease and flour two 8-inch round cake pans. Set aside.
2 Prepare the Cake: Combine coca and boiling water in 2-cup glass measure, stir to dissolve. Allow to cool completely.
3 Cream butter, sugar and jam in a large mixing bowl until light and fluffy. Add eggs one at a time, beating well after each addition. Alternately fold in flour with cocoa mixture, (mixture will be slightly granular) beginning and ending with the flour.
4 Turn batter into prepared pans. Bake in the preheated moderate oven at 350° for 35 minutes or until a wooden pick inserted in the center of the cakes comes out clean. Cool the cakes in the pans on wire racks for 10 minutes. Loosen the cakes around the edges and invert onto racks to cool completely.
5 Prepare the Chocolate Mocha Frosting: Beat butter in a small mixing bowl until smooth and creamy. Gradually add IOX (confectioners') sugar, beating well. Combine cocoa, coffee and milk in a small bowl. Beat until smooth. Add to sugar mixture, beating until well blended and smooth.
6 Place one cake layer on a serving plate. Spread top with frosting. Top with second layer. Spread top and sides with remaining frosting. Decorate cake with glacé cherries and dragées, if you wish.

Best Ever Chocolate Cake

❖
BASIC BUTTER CAKE

Add interest to the cake stall by cooking cakes in differently shaped pans. The following recipe works perfectly using the cake pans and cooking times we have given in the chart (right). Bake according to the chart directions.

- ☐ ¹/₂ cup (1 stick) butter or margarine, softened
- ☐ ³/₄ cup sugar
- ☐ 1 teaspoon vanilla
- ☐ 2 eggs
- ☐ 1¹/₂ cups all-purpose flour, sifted
- ☐ 1¹/₂ teaspoons baking powder
- ☐ ¹/₂ cup milk

1 Preheat the oven to moderate (350°) or hot (400°) according to the size of the cake pan chosen. Grease and flour chosen pan. Set aside.

2 Cream butter and sugar in a small mixing bowl until light and fluffy. Beat in vanilla.

3 Beat in eggs one at a time, beating well after each addition. Combine flour and baking powder on a sheet of waxed paper. Alternately fold in flour with milk, beginning and ending with flour.

4 Bake cake the amount of time specified in the chart (right) for the size of cake pan chosen, until a wooden pick inserted in the center comes out clean. Cool in the pan on a wire rack for 10 minutes; loosen the cake around the edges with a thin metal spatula. Invert onto the wire rack; cool completely.

Basic Butter Cake, Coffee Cake and Apple Cake

PREPARATION
AND COOKING TIMES

PAN SIZE	PREPARATION	TEMPERATURE	COOKING TIME (minutes)
8-inch ring mold	Grease and floured	350°F	40
8-inch round cake pan	Grease and floured	350°F	50
8-inch Bundt ® or Kugelhopf pan	Greased lightly	350°F	40
9 x 5-inch loaf pan	Grease and line with waxed paper	350°F	60
11 x 7 x 2-inch baking pan	Grease and floured	350°F	35
24 regular muffin-pan cups	Paper muffin pan liners	375°F	15

BUTTER CAKE VARIATIONS

COOK'S TIP

1 Make sure your butter and eggs are at room temperature before you start.
2 Use the type of flour specified in the recipe.
3 Bake cake layers in the center of the oven. You can bake more than one layer at a time. Place them on the same shelf, making sure that the pans do not touch each other, the sides or back of the oven, or the oven door when closed. Reverse positions of cake pans halfway through baking.
4 Grease cake pans with melted butter or solid vegetable shortening. Brush evenly over base and sides of pan with a pastry brush then line the base with wax paper or dust with flour, shaking out excess.
5 Don't substitute ingredients.

APPLE CAKE

Spread two-thirds of the cake mixture into the prepared cake pan. Top with $\frac{1}{2}$ cup stewed apples, then remaining cake mixture. Bake according to cake pan size. Let stand 10 minutes before turning out.

ORANGE CAKE

Replace vanilla with 2 teaspoons grated orange zest when creaming butter. Substitute 4 tablespoons orange juice for milk. Bake according to cake pan size. Let stand 5 minutes before turning out.

COFFEE CAKE

Replace vanilla with 1 tablespoon instant coffee dissolved in 1 tablespoon boiling water. Cool, then cream with butter. Bake according to cake pan size. Let stand 5 minutes before turning out.

COCONUT CAKE

Replace vanilla with $\frac{1}{2}$ teaspoon coconut extract and add $\frac{1}{2}$ cup shredded coconut with flour and baking powder. Bake according to pan size. Let stand 5 minutes before turning out.

COOK'S TIP

Test your cake just before the end of baking time. Insert a wooden pick into the thickest part of the cake. If it comes away clean, your cake is done. If there is still cake mixture on the skewer, bake 5 minutes more then test again.

If you prefer, you can gently press the top of cake with your fingertips. When the cake is done, the depression will spring back quickly. When the cake starts to leave the sides of pan, it is also a good indication that cake is done.

BANANA CAKE

Omit milk and add 3 small very ripe mashed bananas to creamed butter and egg mixture. Combine flour, baking powder and 1 teaspoon baking soda and fold into butter and egg mixture. Bake according to pan size. Let stand 5 minutes before turning out.

COOK'S TIP

1   Butter cream frosting can be used as a filling for cakes or made to a thicker consistency for piping.

2   Sift all dry ingredients to remove lumps.

3   Beat butter well before adding IOX (confectioners') sugar.

4   Make sure butter, eggs and cream cheese are at room temperature.

5   To soften cream cheese, leave at room temperature. To soften in the microwave oven, remove foil wrap, place in a microwave-safe dish and cook on HIGH (100%) for 20 seconds.

THE ICING ON THE CAKE

❖

LEMON CREAM CHEESE FROSTING

- ☐ 4 ounces cream cheese
- ☐ 1 teaspoon grated lemon rind
- ☐ 1½ cups IOX (confectioners') sugar, sifted
- ☐ 2 teaspoons lemon juice
- ☐ milk (optional)

Beat cream cheese in a small mixing bowl until creamy. Add lemon rind, IOX (confectioners') sugar and lemon juice. Beat until frosting is a spreadable consistency, adding milk, one teaspoon at a time, if necessary.

❖

CHOCOLATE FROSTING

- ☐ 3 tablespoons butter or margarine, softened
- ☐ 1½ cups IOX (confectioners') sugar, sifted
- ☐ 1 tablespoon unsweetened cocoa powder, sifted
- ☐ 2 tablespoons heavy cream

Beat butter in a small bowl until creamy. Add IOX (confectioners') sugar, cocoa and cream. Beat until frosting is a spreadable consistency, adding additional cream, one teaspoon at a time, if necessary.

Coconut Cake, Banana Cake and Orange Cakes (recipes, page 13)

Cake decorating equipment

❖

COFFEE FROSTING

- ☐ 2 tablespoons butter or margarine, softened
- ☐ 1½ cups IOX (confectioners') sugar, sifted
- ☐ 2 teaspoons instant coffee powder dissolved in 1 tablespoon boiling water
- ☐ milk (optional)

Beat butter in a small mixing bowl until creamy. Add IOX (confectioners') sugar and cooled coffee mixture. Beat until frosting is a spreadable consistency, adding milk, one teaspoon at a time, if necessary.

COOK'S TIP

Always use a IOX (confectioners') sugar mixture unless recipe states otherwise because pure sugar sets as a glaze rather than a frosting. Flavorings that can be used: melted chocolate, orange juice and zest, lemon juice and zest, toppings and sauces, coffee, instant coffee, flavored extracts, coconut.

❖

ORANGE CREAM FROSTING

- ☐ 2 tablespoons cream cheese, softened
- ☐ 2 tablespoons heavy cream
- ☐ 1 teaspoon grated orange rind
- ☐ 1½ cups IOX (confectioners') sugar, sifted

Beat cream cheese, cream and orange rind in a small mixing bowl until creamy. Add IOX (confectioners') sugar. Beat until frosting is a spreadable consistency, adding additional, one teaspoon at a time, if necessary.

QUICK MIX FRUITCAKE

Makes 16 servings

- ☐ ¹/₂ **cup (1 stick) butter or margarine, melted**
- ☐ **1¹/₂ pounds mixed dried fruit**
- ☐ ¹/₂ **cup firmly packed brown sugar**
- ☐ **2 tablespoons raspberry jam**
- ☐ **2 eggs, lightly beaten**
- ☐ ¹/₂ **cup sweet sherry**
- ☐ ³/₄ **cup all-purpose flour, sifted**
- ☐ **3 tablespoons self-rising flour, sifted**
- ☐ ³/₄ **cup blanched almonds**

1 Preheat the oven to slow (325°). Grease a 9-inch tube pan; set aside.
2 Combine butter, fruit, brown sugar, jam, eggs, sherry, all-purpose and self-rising flours in a large bowl. Stir together until all ingredients are well mixed.
3 Turn mixture into the prepared pan. Top with almonds and bake in the preheated slow oven (325°) for 1 hour, 30

minutes. Cool in the pan on a wire rack for 1 hour. Loosen edges, invert onto rack, turn right side up and cool completely. Wrap tightly with aluminum foil and store in an airtight tin.

ZUCCHINI AND WALNUT LOAF

Makes 1 loaf (12 slices)

- ☐ ¹/₂ **cup (1 stick) butter or margarine, softened**
- ☐ **3 tablespoons firmly packed light brown sugar**
- ☐ **3 tablespoons honey**
- ☐ **2 eggs**
- ☐ **2 medium zucchini, grated**
- ☐ ¹/₂ **cup chopped walnuts**
- ☐ **2 cups sifted self-rising flour**
- ☐ **1 teaspoon ground allspice**
- ☐ ¹/₂ **cup buttermilk**

1 Preheat the oven to moderate (350°). Grease and flour a 9 x 5 x 3-inch loaf pan; set aside.
2 Cream butter, sugar and honey in a large mixing bowl until light and fluffy. Beat in eggs; stir in zucchini and walnuts.
3 Combine the flours and allspice on a sheet of waxed paper. Alternately fold in flour with the buttermilk, beginning and ending with the flour.
4 Turn the mixture into the prepared pan. Bake in the preheated moderate oven (350°) for 40 minutes or until a cake tester inserted in the center comes out clean. Cool for 10 minutes in the pan on a wire rack. Turn the loaf out onto the rack and cool completely.

❖
COCONUT COVERED CAKES

Makes 12 squares

- ☐ ¹/₂ **cup (1 stick) butter or margarine, softened**
- ☐ ³/₄ **cup sugar**
- ☐ **1 teaspoon vanilla**
- ☐ **2 eggs**
- ☐ **1 cup self-rising flour, sifted**
- ☐ **1 cup all-purpose flour, sifted**
- ☐ **1 teaspoon baking powder**
- ☐ ¹/₂ **cup milk**

CHOCOLATE FROSTING
- ☐ **3¹/₂ cups IOX (confectioners') sugar, sifted**
- ☐ **3¹/₂ tablespoons unsweetened cocoa powder, sifted**
- ☐ **6-8 tablespoons warm water**
- ☐ **shredded coconut**

1   Preheat the oven to moderate (350°). Grease and flour an 11 x 7 x 1¹/₂-inch baking pan. Set aside.

2   Cream together butter, sugar and vanilla in a small mixing bowl until light and fluffy. Beat in eggs. Combine self-rising

Coconut Covered Cakes

flour, all-purpose flour and baking powder on a sheet of waxed paper. Alternately fold in dry ingredients with milk, beginning and ending with the dry ingredients.

3   Turn batter into prepared pan. Bake in the preheated moderate oven (350°F/180°C) for 30 minutes or until a wooden pick inserted in the center comes out clean. Cool cake in the pan on a wire rack for 10 minutes. Loosen around edges with a thin metal spatula and turn out onto wire rack to cool completely.

4   Prepare the Chocolate Frosting: Combine IOX (confectioners') sugar and cocoa in a large mixing bowl. Add water and beat until smooth. Cut cake into squares and dip into chocolate icing then toss in coconut (See Cook's Tip). Place on greaseproof paper to set.

COOK'S TIP

1   Sprinkle coconut on a sheet of waxed paper. Place a wire rack over a tray or sheet of waxed paper to catch frosting drips.

3 Use tongs or two forks for dipping cake into icing.

4 Drain on the rack for a few minutes, then roll in coconut.

❖
GINGERBREAD FAMILY

Makes 4 families

COOKIES
- ☐ ¹/₂ **cup (1 stick) butter or margarine, softened**
- ☐ ¹/₂ **cup firmly packed brown sugar**
- ☐ **2 tablespoons honey**
- ☐ **1 egg**
- ☐ **1¹/₄ cups all-purpose flour, sifted**
- ☐ **1¹/₂ cups self-rising flour, sifted and divided**
- ☐ **1 teaspoon baking soda**
- ☐ **1 tablespoon ground ginger**

ROYAL ICING
- ☐ **meringue powder**
- ☐ **food coloring**

1   Preheat oven to moderate (350°). Grease 2 large cookie sheets. Set aside.
2   Cream butter, brown sugar and honey in a small mixing bowl until light and fluffy. Beat in egg. Combine 1 cup all-purpose flour, self-rising flour and ginger on sheet of waxed paper. Gradually fold into butter mixture.
3   Sprinkle remaining all-purpose flour onto a smooth surface and knead mixture until soft but not sticky. Wrap the dough in plastic wrap and chill for 30 minutes. Divide dough into four portions. Roll out one-fourth of the dough, keeping the remainder of the dough refrigerated, on the floured surface to a ¹/₈-inch thickness.
4   Cut into gingerbread people shapes using two large (4 to 4¹/₂-inch) cutters and four small (2¹/₂ to 3-inch) cutters. Using a spatula, carefully lift gingerbread figures onto prepared cookie sheets. Re-roll remaining scraps and cut out.
5   Bake in the preheated moderate oven (350°) for 10 minutes or until lightly golden. Cool on cookie sheets set on wire racks for 1 to 2 minutes. Remove to wire racks to cool completely.
6   Prepare 1 recipe Royal Frosting according to directions on label of container of meringue powder. One level tablespoon will frost one 4 x 3-inch cookie; one level teaspoon will frost one 3 x 2-inch cookie. Divide frostings into small bowls. Tint with

Gingerbread Family

Roll out dough to $\frac{1}{8}$-inch thickness.

Cut out shapes with gingerbread cookie cutters.

desired food colorings. Keep bowls covered with damp paper towelling to prevent drying out.

7   Spoon frosting into pastry bags fitted with decorative tips and decorate as desired.

Note: *We prefer using dried meringue powder for uncooked frosting due to the increased concern of the presence of salmonella bacteria in raw eggs. Meringue powder is available in stores where decorating and baking supplies are sold.*

COOK'S TIP

When making cookies, butter should always be slightly softened. Do not overbeat cookie dough.

Cookie sheets, instead of trays with sides, are best for baking. Position cookies in top half of the oven for baking. When positioning cookies on the sheet, allow 1½-2 inches between each cookie.

Cookies should be browned to an even color.

Pipe on facial features and clothes.

❖ HONEY MALT BARS ❖

Makes 20 bars
- ☐ **2 cups self-rising flour, sifted**
- ☐ **1 cup rolled oats**
- ☐ **1 cup flaked coconut**
- ☐ **3 cups crushed natural high fiber bran cereal**
- ☐ **1 cup firmly packed light brown sugar**
- ☐ **1 cup (2 sticks) butter or margarine, melted**
- ☐ **¹⁄₄ cup honey**

MOCHA FROSTIN[G]
- ☐ **1 cup IOX (con[fectioners']) sifted**
- ☐ **2 teaspoons ur[ ] powder**
- ☐ **2 teaspoons ins[ ]**
- ☐ **1¹⁄₂ teaspoons b[ ]**
- ☐ **1 tablespoon wa[ ]**

1   Preheat the ove[n]
Grease a 15 x 10-inch [ ]
2   Prepare the bars [ ]
oats, coconut, bran c[ ]
large mixing bowl. M[ ]
Blend together butter [ ]
into dry ingredients.
3   Press mixture int[o]
4   Bake in the prehe[ated]
(350°) for 35 minutes, [ ]
pick inserted into the [ ]
clean. Remove to a [ ]
completely.
5   Prepare Frosting: [ ]
(confectioners') suga[r]
powder and butter in th[e]
boiler or a small bowl. Be[ ]
top of double boiler or bow[l]
of hot (not boiling) wate[r]
frosting is of spreading c[ ]
6   Spread the top of the co[ ]
Frosting and let sit until firm enough to cut.

❖ MUESLI BARS ❖

Makes 36 bars
- ☐ **1¹⁄₂ cups five-grain muesli cereal**
- ☐ **¹⁄₂ cup flaked coconut**
- ☐ **¹⁄₂ cup whole wheat flour, sifted**
- ☐ **¹⁄₂ cup pine nuts**
- ☐ **³⁄₄ cup golden raisins**
- ☐ **3 tablespoons sesame seeds**
- ☐ **¹⁄₂ cup firmly packed brown sugar**
- ☐ **¹⁄₂ cup (1 stick) butter or margarine, melted**
- ☐ **2 tablespoons honey**
- ☐ **2 eggs, lightly beaten**

1   Preheat the oven to moderate (350°). Grease a 11 x 7 x 1¹⁄₂-inch baking pan.
2   Combine muesli, coconut, flour, nuts, raisins, sesame seeds and sugar in a large mixing bowl; set aside. Blend together butter, honey and eggs in a small bowl and stir into dry ingredients.
3   Press mixture into the prepared pan. Bake in the preheated moderate oven

Clockwise from top: Honey Malt Bars, Hazelnut Fingers, Muesli Bars, Almond Cookies, Chocolate Chip Cookies

---

(350°) for 20 minutes or until a wooden pick inserted in the center comes out clean. Remove to a wire rack to cool completely.

❖ ALMOND COOKIES ❖

Makes 36
- ☐ **¹⁄₂ cup (1 stick) butter or margarine, softened**
- ☐ **1 cup sugar**
- ☐ **¹⁄₂ teaspoon almond extract**
- ☐ **1 egg**
- ☐ **1 cup all-purpose flour, sifted**
- ☐ **1 cup self-rising flour, sifted**
- ☐ **¹⁄₂ cup shredded coconut**
- ☐ **¹⁄₂ cup chopped glacé cherries**
- ☐ **1 cup chopped almonds**

[1]   Preheat the oven to moderate (350°). [2] Beat butter and sugar in a small mixing [bo]wl until creamy. Beat in almond extract [and] egg. Fold in flour, coconut and cherries [unti]l well blended. Cover and refrigerate [2] hours.
[3]   Roll heaped teaspoonfuls of dough [into] balls. Dip one half of each ball into [chop]ped almonds and place almond side [up o]n a greased cookie sheet 2 inches [apar]t. Flatten each biscuit slightly and [bake] in the preheated moderate oven [(350°)] for 12 minutes or until golden. [Cool] on cookie sheets set on wire racks for [1 min]ute. Remove to wire racks and cool [comp]letely.

❖ HAZELNUT FINGERS ❖

[Makes] 45
- ☐ **[2] egg whites**
- ☐ **[ ] cup sugar**
- ☐ **[ ] cup ground hazelnuts**
- ☐ **[ ] teaspoon almond extract**
- ☐ **3 tablespoons cornstarch**
- ☐ **3 tablespoons all-purpose flour**
- ☐ **4 squares (1 ounce each) unsweetened chocolate**
- ☐ **1¹⁄₂ tablespoons solid vegetable shortening**

1   Preheat oven to moderate (350°).
2   Beat egg whites in a small mixing bowl until soft peaks form. Add sugar 2 tablespoons at a time, beating well after each addition until meringue stands in firm peaks.
3   Fold in hazelnuts, almond extract, cornstarch and flour. Spoon mixture into a pastry bag fitted with a writing tip. Pipe 2-inch lengths onto greased cookie sheets. Bake in the preheated oven (350°) for 10 minutes. Cool on cookie sheets set on wire racks for 1 minute. Remove to wire racks and cool completely.
4   Combine chocolate and vegetable shortening in the top of a double boiler or a small bowl set over a saucepan of hot (not boiling) water. Stir occasionally until chocolate is melted and mixture is smooth. Dip cooled cookie ends in chocolate mixture. Place on aluminum foil to set.

❖ CHOCOLATE CHIP ❖ COOKIES

Makes 36 cookies
- ☐ **¹⁄₂ cup butter or margarine, softened**
- ☐ **¹⁄₂ cup sugar**
- ☐ **¹⁄₂ cup packed light brown sugar**
- ☐ **¹⁄₂ teaspoon coconut extract**
- ☐ **1 egg**
- ☐ **³⁄₄ cup all-purpose flour, sifted**
- ☐ **¹⁄₂ cup coconut**
- ☐ **¹⁄₂ cup (4 ounces) chocolate chips**
- ☐ **4 squares (1 ounce each) unsweetened chocolate, melted**

1   Preheat the oven to moderate (350°).
2   Beat butter, sugars and coconut extract until creamy. Beat in egg. Fold in flour, coconut and chocolate chips.
3   Drop teaspoonfuls of dough onto large greased cookie sheet about 2 inches apart. Bake in preheated moderate oven (350°) for 15 minutes. Cool on cookie sheets set on wire racks for 1 minute. Remove to wire racks and cool completely.
4   Spoon melted chocolate into a pastry bag fitted with a small writing tip. Pipe 3 thin lines over top of each cookie.

❖ ORANGE SHORTBREAD ❖

Makes 20 squares
- ☐ **1 cup (2 sticks) butter or margarine, softened**
- ☐ **¹⁄₂ cup plus 1 tablespoon sugar**
- ☐ **1 tablespoon orange juice**
- ☐ **1 teaspoon grated orange rind**
- ☐ **2¹⁄₂ cups all-purpose flour, sifted**
- ☐ **¹⁄₄ cup cornstarch**

1   Preheat the oven to moderate (350°). Grease an 8-inch square cake pan.
2   Beat butter and ¹⁄₂ cup sugar in a small mixing bowl until creamy. Beat in orange juice and rind, combine flours and cornstarch on a sheet of waxed paper. Fold into butter mixture until well blended and smooth.
3   Spread mixture into prepared pan. Mark into squares, prick with a fork and sprinkle over remaining sugar. Bake in the preheated moderate oven (350°) for 40 minutes or until a wooden pick inserted in the center comes out clean. Remove to a wire rack to cool completely.

MICROWAVE IT

When making Hazelnut Fingers, place chocolate and vegetable shortening in a microwave-safe bowl. Microwave at full power (100%) for 1-2 minutes or until chocolate is melted. Stir after every 30 seconds. Be careful not to overcook, as chocolate will burn easily.

CHOCOLATE CURLS

- ■ Melt 2 or 3 ounces fine-quality bittersweet chocolate in the microwave or over a double boiler.
- ■ Pour onto the clean underside of a baking sheet. Using a long metal spatula, spread chocolate in a thin layer. Refrigerate until nearly set.
- ■ Holding a paint scraper at a 45-degree angle, draw it gently across the chocolate to form long curls. Transfer curls to a plate and refrigerate. Use as a garnish with your favorite dessert.

CHOCOLATE ECLAIRS

When making these to sell at a fair or bazaar do not fill them until the last possible moment and remember do not let them sit in the sun. If possible just display one or two trays at a time and keep the others in an insulated container under the counter. Alternately, just make the cases and sell them unfilled. You may like to attach a label with the recipe for the filling.

Makes about 8

ECLAIR DOUGH
- [ ] $^1/_4$ cup ($^1/_2$ stick) butter, chopped
- [ ] 1 cup water
- [ ] 1 cup all-purpose flour
- [ ] 4 eggs, lightly beaten

BRANDY CREAM FILLING
- [ ] $1^1/_2$ cups heavy cream
- [ ] 2 tablespoons IOX (confectioners') sugar
- [ ] 3 tablespoons brandy

CHOCOLATE TOPPING
- [ ] 4 ounces milk chocolate, melted
- [ ] 1 tablespoon butter, melted

1   Preheat the oven to hot (400°). Line cookie sheets with nonstick parchment paper.
2   To make éclairs, melt butter in a medium saucepan, add water and bring to a boil over a medium heat. Add flour all at once and stir vigorously over heat until mixture leaves the sides of pan and forms a smooth ball. Transfer mixture to a bowl and set aside to cool for 10 minutes. Add eggs, one at a time, beating well after each addition.
3   Spoon batter into a large pastry bag fitted with a $^1/_2$-inch plain tube and pipe 4-inch lengths onto cookie sheets. Bake in the preheated hot oven (400°) for 10 minutes, then reduce oven temperature to moderate (350°) and bake for 25 minutes longer. Turn off heat and allow cases to cool in oven with door open.
4   To make filling, place cream, IOX (confectioners') sugar and brandy in a bowl and whip until soft peaks form. Split éclairs lengthwise and fill with Brandy Cream Filling.
5   For topping, combine melted chocolate and butter and drizzle over top of éclairs.

Chocolate Eclairs

LEMON AND LIME BARS

Makes 30

- [ ] $^1/_2$ cup (1 stick) butter or margarine
- [ ] 1 cup all-purpose flour
- [ ] $^1/_2$ cup IOX (confectioners') sugar

LEMON AND LIME TOPPING
- [ ] 2 eggs, lightly beaten
- [ ] 1 cup superfine sugar
- [ ] 4 teaspoons all-purpose flour
- [ ] 4 teaspoons lemon juice
- [ ] 3 tablespoons lime juice
- [ ] 1 teaspoon finely grated lemon rind

1   Preheat the oven to moderate (375°). Grease and line a shallow 7 x 11-inch cake pan.
2   Place butter, flour and IOX (confectioners') sugar in a food processor and process to form a soft dough. Turn dough onto a lightly floured surface and knead lightly. Press dough into pan. Bake in the preheated moderate oven (375°) for 20 minutes or until firm. Cool in pan.
3   To make topping, place eggs, sugar, flour, lemon juice, lime juice and lemon rind in a bowl and mix until combined. Pour over cooked layer and bake for 25-30 minutes longer or until topping is firm. Refrigerate until cold, then cut into bars.

CINNAMON COOKIES

Makes 25-30

- [ ] $^1/_2$ cup (1 stick) butter
- [ ] $^1/_2$ cup IOX (confectioners') sugar
- [ ] 2 teaspoons vanilla extract
- [ ] 1 cup all-purpose flour
- [ ] 1 tablespoon ground cinnamon
- [ ] 2 tablespoons superfine sugar

1   Preheat the oven to moderate (350°). Lightly grease cookie sheets.
2   Place butter, IOX (confectioners') sugar and vanilla in a bowl and beat until light and fluffy. Gradually, stir flour into butter mixture and mix to make a soft dough.
3   Using floured hands roll teaspoons of dough into balls and place 2-inch apart on cookie sheets. Bake in the preheated moderate oven (350°) for 10-12 minutes or until cookies are golden. Transfer cookies to wire racks. Combine cinnamon and superfine sugar, sprinkle over hot cookies and allow to cool.

SHORTBREAD CREAMS

Makes 24

- [ ] 1 cup (2 sticks) butter, softened
- [ ] $^1/_3$ cup IOX (confectioners') sugar, sifted
- [ ] 1 cup cornstarch
- [ ] 1 cup all-purpose flour

LEMON CREAM FILLING
- [ ] $^1/_4$ cup ($^1/_2$ stick) butter, softened
- [ ] $^1/_2$ cup IOX (confectioners') sugar
- [ ] 2 teaspoons finely grated lemon rind
- [ ] 1 tablespoon lemon juice

1   Preheat the oven to moderate (350°). Grease cookie sheets.
2   Place butter and IOX (confectioners') sugar in a bowl and beat until light and fluffy. Sift together cornstarch and flour and stir into butter mixture.
3   Spoon mixture into a pastry bag fitted with a large star nozzle and pipe small rosettes onto cookie sheets, leaving space between each rosette. Bake in the preheated moderate oven (350°) for 15-20 minutes or until just golden. Allow cookies to cool on sheets.
4   To make filling, place butter in a bowl and beat until light and fluffy. Gradually add IOX (confectioners') sugar and beat until creamy. Stir in lemon rind and lemon juice. Sandwich together with filling.

GINGER SNAPS

Makes 45

- [ ] 1 cup firmly packed brown sugar
- [ ] 1 tablespoon ground ginger
- [ ] 2 cups all-purpose flour
- [ ] $^1/_2$ cup (1 stick) butter
- [ ] 1 cup light molasses
- [ ] 1 teaspoon baking soda

1   Preheat the oven to moderate (350°). Grease cookie sheets.
2   Sift sugar, ginger and flour together into a bowl. Place butter and molasses in a saucepan and cook over a low heat, stirring, until butter melts. Stir in baking soda. Pour molasses mixture into dry ingredients and mix until smooth.
3   Drop teaspoons of mixture onto greased cookie sheets and bake in the preheated moderate oven (350°) for 10-12 mintues or until golden. Remove from oven, loosen cookies with a spatula and allow to cool on sheets.

FRUITY CEREAL SQUARES

Dried fruit, puffed rice cereal, coconut, nuts and honey – just reading the ingredients you know that this slice is going to be delicious.

Makes 30

- ☐ **3 cups unsweetened puffed rice cereal**
- ☐ **1 cup bran flake cereal, crumbled**
- ☐ **1 cup slivered almonds, toasted**
- ☐ **1 cup dried apricots, chopped**
- ☐ **$^1/_2$ cup candied pineapple, chopped**
- ☐ **$^1/_2$ cup crystallized ginger or preserved ginger in syrup, chopped**
- ☐ **$^1/_2$ cup seeded raisins, chopped**
- ☐ **1 cup golden seedless raisins**
- ☐ **$^1/_2$ cup (1 stick) butter or margarine**
- ☐ **$^1/_2$ cup heavy cream**
- ☐ **$^1/_2$ cup honey**
- ☐ **$^1/_3$ cup granulated brown (raw or demerara) sugar**

1   Place rice cereal, bran cereal, almonds, apricots, pineapple, ginger, seeded raisins and golden seedless raisins in a large bowl, mix to combine and set aside.

2   Place butter, cream, honey and sugar in a saucepan and cook over a low heat, stirring constantly, until sugar dissolves and butter melts. Bring to a boil, then reduce heat and simmer for 5 minutes or until mixture thickens slightly.

3   Pour honey mixture into dry ingredients and mix well to combine. Press mixture into a greased and lined shallow 7 x 11-inch cake pan. Refrigerate until firm, then cut into squares.

DATE BARS

Makes 30

- ☐ **$^3/_4$ cup evaporated milk**
- ☐ **$^3/_4$ cup pitted dates, chopped**
- ☐ **$^1/_2$ cup (1 stick) butter or margarine, softened**
- ☐ **$^1/_2$ cup superfine sugar**
- ☐ **1 teaspoon vanilla extract**
- ☐ **1 cup flour, sifted with $^1/_2$ teaspoon baking powder**
- ☐ **$^2/_3$ cup pecans, chopped**

1   Preheat the oven to moderate (350°). Grease and line a 9-inch square cake pan. Place evaporated milk in a saucepan and bring to a boil over a low heat. Place dates in a bowl, pour over hot milk and set aside to cool.

2   Place butter, sugar and vanilla in a bowl and beat until light and fluffy. Mix flour and date mixtures, alternately, into butter mixture, then fold in pecans. Spoon mixture into the prepared cake pan and bake in preheated moderate oven (350°) for 25-30 minutes or until firm. Stand in pan for 5 minutes before turning onto a wire rack to cool. Cut into bars.

GINGER CRUNCH

Makes 30

- ☐ **$^1/_2$ cup (1 stick) butter or margarine**
- ☐ **$^3/_4$ cup sugar**
- ☐ **$^1/_2$ cup sweetened condensed milk**
- ☐ **4 teaspoons light molasses**
- ☐ **2$^1/_2$ cups crisp gingersnap cookie crumbs**
- ☐ **$^1/_4$ cup pecans, finely chopped**
- ☐ **2 tablespoons finely chopped crystallized ginger or preserved ginger in syrup**

1   Place butter, sugar, condensed milk and molasses in a saucepan and cook over a medium heat, stirring constantly, until mixture is smooth. Bring to a boil, then reduce heat and simmer for 3-4 minutes or until mixture thickens slightly.

2   Place cookie crumbs, pecans and ginger in a bowl, pour in condensed milk mixture and mix until well combined. Press mixture into a lined shallow 9-inch square cake pan and refrigerate until set. Cut into bars.

LEMON AND PISTACHIO NUT BARS

Topped with pistachio nuts and candied citrus peel this slice tastes as good as it looks.

Makes 30

- ☐ **2$^1/_2$ cups plain cookies crumbs**
- ☐ **$^3/_4$ cup pistachio nuts, chopped**
- ☐ **2 teaspoons finely grated lemon rind**
- ☐ **$^1/_2$ cup sweetened condensed milk**
- ☐ **$^1/_2$ cup (1 stick) butter or margarine, melted**

LEMON PISTACHIO TOPPING
- ☐ **$^1/_2$ cup cream cheese, softened**
- ☐ **$^1/_2$ cup IOX (confectioners') sugar, sifted**
- ☐ **2 teaspoons lemon juice**
- ☐ **$^1/_4$ cup diced mixed candied citrus peel, finely chopped**
- ☐ **1 tablespoon chopped pistachio nuts**

1   Place cookie crumbs, pistachio nuts, lemon rind, condensed milk and butter in a bowl and mix to combine. Press mixture into a greased and lined shallow 7 x 11-inch cake pan.

2   To make topping, place cream cheese and IOX (confectioners') sugar in a mixing bowl and beat until fluffy. Beat in lemon juice and spread over mixture in cake pan. Sprinkle with citrus peel and pistachio nuts and refrigerate until topping is firm. Cut into bars.

Fruity Cereal Squares, Date Bars

Sweet temptations

A child's delight – this booth is a treasure trove of candy apples, honeycomb, fudge, and other sugar-coated delights !

Candy-making can be a difficult task – so enlist the help of experienced candy-makers or good cooks. For consistent quality, everyone must use reliable, well-tested recipes. When you have decided on the variety of candies you and your team are going to make, compile master plans with all the recipes, cooking, storing and delivery instructions. Give each candy-maker a copy, highlighting the recipes he or she has agreed to make.

Package your candies at a central point a day or two before the fair. Wrap them in clear plastic boxes, cellophane bags or tissue paper. Pretty tins and covered chocolate boxes are also excellent for wrapping — but start collecting them early to be sure you have enough. Decorate your packages with colorful curling ribbon and silk flowers.

PRICES

Keep your "manufacturing" costs to a minimum so that you can keep your prices below retail. Make sure there is a good selection of inexpensive treats for children. Adults love to indulge in their favorite confectionery and will usually pay that little bit extra for beautiful wrapping and presentation.

DECORATION

Decorating the candy booth is a treat in itself. Make it look delicious by winding ribbon around the support poles and taping bags of candies onto them. Hang candy apples on strings from the top of the stall and use baskets and shelving to add interest to the display.

COOK'S TIP

Use a deep, heavy-based saucepan made of aluminium, copper or stainless steel.

Dissolve the sugar in the water or liquid very slowly over low heat. Do not allow it to boil until sugar is completely dissolved. After boiling begins, remove any crystals that form on the sides of pan with a clean brush dipped in warm water. Do not stir after boiling point is reached unless recipe states otherwise.

Most candies are better when made in dry, cool weather as high humidity can affect cooking times and temperatures. Temperature should be 1-2 degrees higher on very humid days.

Try not to scrape dregs of candy from the pan as the crystallization rate between this and the free flowing portion will differ because of the greater amount of heat applied to the base of the pan.

❖

CANDY APPLES

The thick wooden skewers used for the candy apples can be purchased from cake decorating suppliers. Dip carefully — air bubbles form if you dip too quickly.

Makes 10 apples

- ☐ **4 cups sugar**
- ☐ **1 cup (2 sticks) butter or margarine**
- ☐ **$\frac{1}{4}$ cup white vinegar**
- ☐ **$\frac{1}{4}$ cup boiling water**
- ☐ **$\frac{1}{2}$ teaspoon red food coloring**
- ☐ **10 small green apples, washed and dried**
- ☐ **10 thick wooden skewers**

1 Combine sugar, butter, vinegar, boiling water and food coloring in a large heavy metal saucepan. Cook over a low heat, stirring until sugar dissolves.

2 Increase heat and boil without stirring for about 10 minutes or until mixture reaches the hard crack stage or 300°F on a candy thermometer. Remove from heat and allow bubbles to subside.

3 Pierce apples through the center with the wooden skewers. With the pan tilted to one side carefully dip an apple into the toffee and twist slowly to completely coat. Remove apple slowly and twirl over pan to remove excess toffee. Dip coated apple into iced water to harden toffee then place on a slightly oiled cookie sheet to set. Repeat with remaining apples. If toffee becomes too thick to work with, place over a moderate heat.

COOK'S TIP

Candy apples must be made as close to the serving time as possible and stored in airtight containers to prevent them from sweating. Fudge should be kept away from sunlight. Chocolate items should be stored in the refrigerator until needed.

Candy Apples

Pierce apples through the centre with wooden skewers.

With the pan tilted to one side carefully dip apple.

Dip coated apple into icewater.

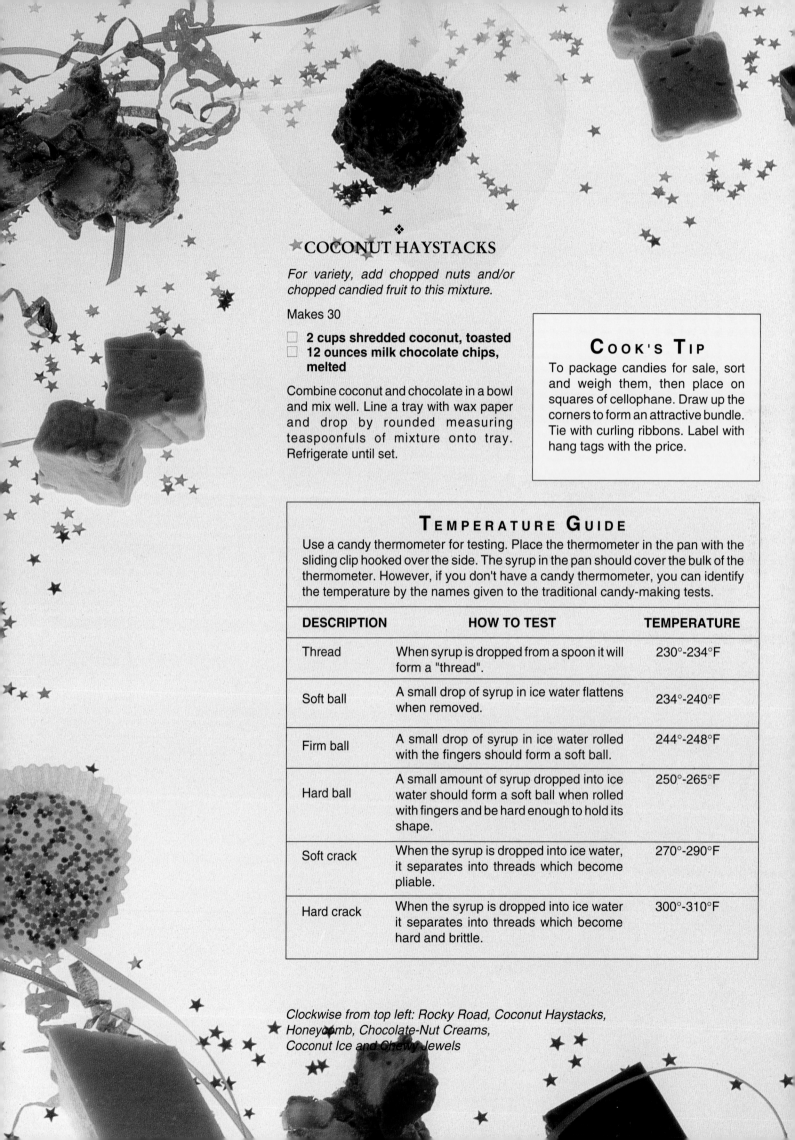

❖
✶COCONUT HAYSTACKS

For variety, add chopped nuts and/or chopped candied fruit to this mixture.

Makes 30

- [ ] **2 cups shredded coconut, toasted**
- [ ] **12 ounces milk chocolate chips, melted**

Combine coconut and chocolate in a bowl and mix well. Line a tray with wax paper and drop by rounded measuring teaspoonfuls of mixture onto tray. Refrigerate until set.

COOK'S TIP

To package candies for sale, sort and weigh them, then place on squares of cellophane. Draw up the corners to form an attractive bundle. Tie with curling ribbons. Label with hang tags with the price.

TEMPERATURE GUIDE

Use a candy thermometer for testing. Place the thermometer in the pan with the sliding clip hooked over the side. The syrup in the pan should cover the bulk of the thermometer. However, if you don't have a candy thermometer, you can identify the temperature by the names given to the traditional candy-making tests.

DESCRIPTION	HOW TO TEST	TEMPERATURE
Thread	When syrup is dropped from a spoon it will form a "thread".	230°-234°F
Soft ball	A small drop of syrup in ice water flattens when removed.	234°-240°F
Firm ball	A small drop of syrup in ice water rolled with the fingers should form a soft ball.	244°-248°F
Hard ball	A small amount of syrup dropped into ice water should form a soft ball when rolled with fingers and be hard enough to hold its shape.	250°-265°F
Soft crack	When the syrup is dropped into ice water, it separates into threads which become pliable.	270°-290°F
Hard crack	When the syrup is dropped into ice water it separates into threads which become hard and brittle.	300°-310°F

Clockwise from top left: Rocky Road, Coconut Haystacks, Honeycomb, Chocolate-Nut Creams, Coconut Ice and Chewy Jewels

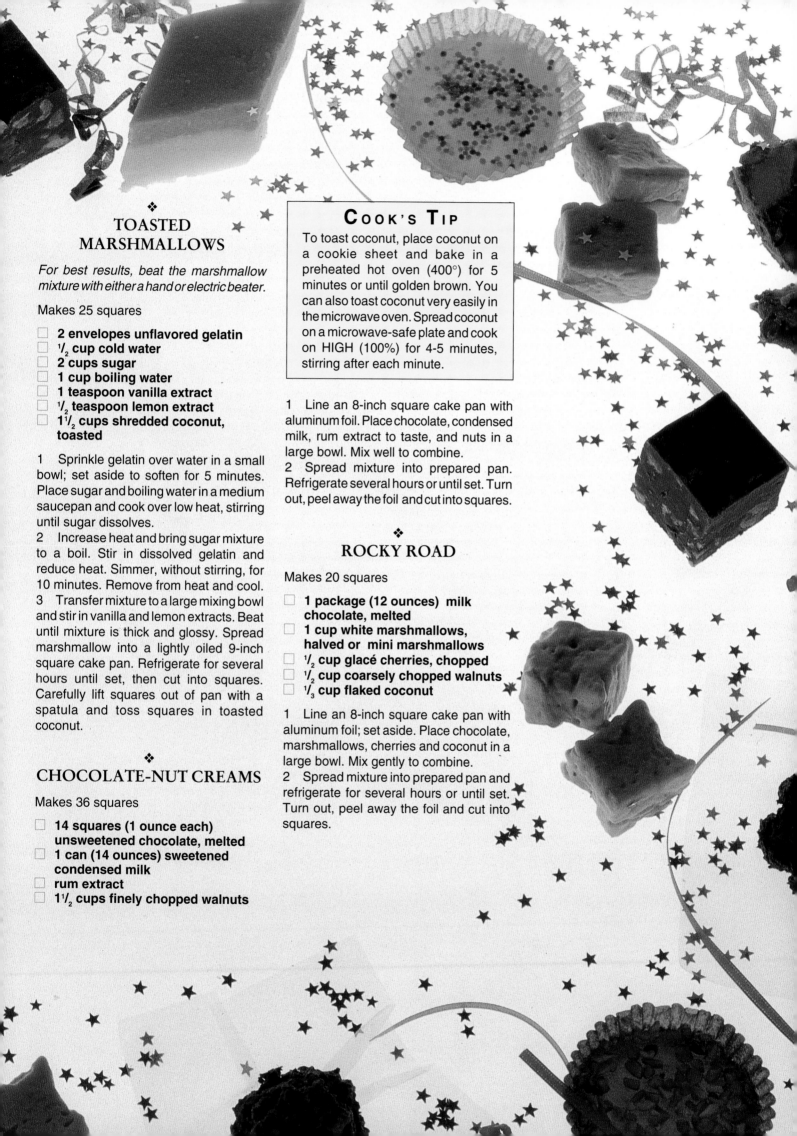

TOASTED MARSHMALLOWS

For best results, beat the marshmallow mixture with either a hand or electric beater.

Makes 25 squares

- ☐ **2 envelopes unflavored gelatin**
- ☐ **1/2 cup cold water**
- ☐ **2 cups sugar**
- ☐ **1 cup boiling water**
- ☐ **1 teaspoon vanilla extract**
- ☐ **1/2 teaspoon lemon extract**
- ☐ **1 1/2 cups shredded coconut, toasted**

1 Sprinkle gelatin over water in a small bowl; set aside to soften for 5 minutes. Place sugar and boiling water in a medium saucepan and cook over low heat, stirring until sugar dissolves.

2 Increase heat and bring sugar mixture to a boil. Stir in dissolved gelatin and reduce heat. Simmer, without stirring, for 10 minutes. Remove from heat and cool.

3 Transfer mixture to a large mixing bowl and stir in vanilla and lemon extracts. Beat until mixture is thick and glossy. Spread marshmallow into a lightly oiled 9-inch square cake pan. Refrigerate for several hours until set, then cut into squares. Carefully lift squares out of pan with a spatula and toss squares in toasted coconut.

CHOCOLATE-NUT CREAMS

Makes 36 squares

- ☐ **14 squares (1 ounce each) unsweetened chocolate, melted**
- ☐ **1 can (14 ounces) sweetened condensed milk**
- ☐ **rum extract**
- ☐ **1 1/2 cups finely chopped walnuts**

COOK'S TIP

To toast coconut, place coconut on a cookie sheet and bake in a preheated hot oven (400°) for 5 minutes or until golden brown. You can also toast coconut very easily in the microwave oven. Spread coconut on a microwave-safe plate and cook on HIGH (100%) for 4-5 minutes, stirring after each minute.

1 Line an 8-inch square cake pan with aluminum foil. Place chocolate, condensed milk, rum extract to taste, and nuts in a large bowl. Mix well to combine.

2 Spread mixture into prepared pan. Refrigerate several hours or until set. Turn out, peel away the foil and cut into squares.

ROCKY ROAD

Makes 20 squares

- ☐ **1 package (12 ounces) milk chocolate, melted**
- ☐ **1 cup white marshmallows, halved or mini marshmallows**
- ☐ **1/2 cup glacé cherries, chopped**
- ☐ **1/2 cup coarsely chopped walnuts**
- ☐ **1/3 cup flaked coconut**

1 Line an 8-inch square cake pan with aluminum foil; set aside. Place chocolate, marshmallows, cherries and coconut in a large bowl. Mix gently to combine.

2 Spread mixture into prepared pan and refrigerate for several hours or until set. Turn out, peel away the foil and cut into squares.

ALMOND TRUFFLES

Makes about 20 candies

- ☐ **1 square (1 ounce) unsweetened chocolate**
- ☐ **4 ounces ($^1/_2$ cup) marzipan**
- ☐ **2 tablespoons ground almonds**
- ☐ **2 teaspoons vanilla extract**
- ☐ **1 teaspoon sweet creamy sherry**
- ☐ **finely chopped almonds**

1   Melt chocolate in the top of a double boiler or a small bowl set over hot (not boiling) water. Stir in marzipan, ground almonds, vanilla and sherry.
2   Knead mixture well and form into small balls. Roll in chopped almonds, cover and refrigerate several hours or until firm.

APRICOT BALLS

These apricot balls can be made up to one week in advance. Store them in an airtight container between layers of waxed paper.

Makes 30 balls

- ☐ **$^1/_2$ cup dried apricots, finely chopped**
- ☐ **$^1/_2$ cup pitted prunes, finely chopped**
- ☐ **$^1/_4$ cup raisins, finely chopped**
- ☐ **$3^1/_2$ tablespoons Grand Marnier or orange juice**
- ☐ **2 teaspoons grated orange rind**
- ☐ **$1^1/_3$ cups shredded coconut**
- ☐ **$^3/_4$ cup chopped almonds**
- ☐ **$^3/_4$ cup sugar**

1   Place apricots, prunes, raisins and 3 tablespoons Grand Marnier in a medium size bowl and let stand for 1 hour.
2   Combine chopped fruit with orange rind, $2^1/_2$ tablespoons coconut and nuts. Form mixture into bite-size balls adding remaining Grand Marnier if necessary to make the mixture easier to shape. Mix together remaining coconut and sugar, and roll apricot balls in this mixture to coat.

CHEWY JEWELS

You can make these candies up to a week in advance and store them in airtight containers, but do not freeze.

Makes 12 candies

- ☐ **2 cups sugar**
- ☐ **1 cup water**
- ☐ **$2^1/_2$ tablespoons butter or margarine**
- ☐ **2 teaspoons vinegar**
- ☐ **2 teaspoons honey**
- ☐ **chopped nuts**

1   Place sugar, water, butter, vinegar and honey in a medium saucepan and cook over a low heat, stirring until sugar dissolves.
2   Increase heat and boil without stirring for about 12 minutes until mixture is golden brown and reaches the hard crack stage or 310°F on a candy thermometer . Remove from heat and allow bubbles to subside.
3   Pour toffee into paper candy cases and sprinkle with chopped nuts.

HONEYCOMB

Makes 30 squares

- ☐ **1 cup sugar**
- ☐ **1 tablespoon honey**
- ☐ **1 tablespoon vinegar**
- ☐ **1 tablespoon butter**
- ☐ **$^1/_2$ teaspoon baking soda**

1   Combine sugar, honey, vinegar and butter in a heavy metal saucepan and cook over medium heat, stirring until sugar dissolves.
2   Increase heat and boil without stirring until mixture reaches hard crack stage or 300°F on a candy thermometer and a few drops of mixture snap and crackle and immediately harden when dropped into ice water.
3   Remove pan from heat and add baking soda, stirring until mixture swells. Pour into a lightly oiled 9-inch square cake pan. When cold, break into pieces.

ALMOND-PECAN BRITTLE

Makes 25 squares

- ☐ **1 cup whole blanched almonds**
- ☐ **¹/₂ cup pecans**
- ☐ **1¹/₂ cups sugar**
- ☐ **³/₄ cup firmly packed light brown sugar**
- ☐ **¹/₂ cup honey**
- ☐ **¹/₂ cup water**
- ☐ **¹/₄ cup (2 tablespoons) butter or margarine**
- ☐ **¹/₄ teaspoon baking soda**

1 Preheat the oven to moderate (350°).
2 Combine almonds and pecans on a large cookie sheet and bake in the preheated moderate oven (350°) for 5 minutes or until light golden brown. Remove from oven and set aside.
3 Combine sugars, honey and water in a heavy metal saucepan and cook over medium heat, stirring until sugar dissolves. Add butter. Bring to a boil. Boil, without stirring, until mixture reaches hard crack stage 300°F on a candy thermometer.
4 Stir in baking soda and toasted nuts. Pour into a lightly oiled 9-inch square cake pan. When almost set, cut into squares.

RUM BALLS

Makes about 60 balls

- ☐ **4 cups plain cake crumbs**
- ☐ **³/₄ cup finely chopped raisins**
- ☐ **1 can (14 ounces) sweetened condensed milk**
- ☐ **2 cups shredded coconut**
- ☐ **2 teaspoons grated lemon rind**
- ☐ **1 tablespoon lemon juice**
- ☐ **1 tablespoon unsweetened cocoa powder**
- ☐ **2 tablespoons rum or rum extract**
- ☐ **chocolate sprinkles**

1 Combine cake crumbs, raisins, condensed milk, coconut, lemon rind, juice, cocoa powder and rum in a large bowl and mix well.
2 Form mixture into small balls and toss to coat in chocolate sprinkles. Cover and refrigerate until firm.

CREAMY CARAMELS

Makes 25

- ☐ **1 cup firmly packed brown sugar**
- ☐ **2 tablespoons water**
- ☐ **¹/₄ cup (¹/₂ stick) butter or margarine**
- ☐ **¹/₄ teaspoon vanilla**
- ☐ **3 tablespoons heavy cream**

1 Place sugar and water in a heavy metal saucepan and cook over medium heat, stirring until sugar dissolves.
2 Add butter, vanilla and cream, increase heat and boil, without stirring, until mixture reaches hard ball stage or 265°F on a candy thermometer. A few drops will form a soft ball when dropped into iced water.
3 Pour caramel into a lightly oiled 8-inch square cake pan. When almost set, cut into squares.

Clockwise from left: Almond Truffles, Almond-Pecan Brittle, Apricot Balls and Rum Balls

FRUIT AND NUT CARAMELS

Makes about 70 pieces

- ☐ $1/2$ cup glacé cherries, chopped
- ☐ $1/4$ cup chopped candied apricots
- ☐ $1/2$ cup whole mixed nuts
- ☐ 1 cup sugar
- ☐ $1/3$ cup butter or margarine
- ☐ 2 tablespoons honey
- ☐ $1/3$ cup liquid glucose
- ☐ $1/2$ cup sweetened condensed milk

1   Spread cherries, apricots and nuts evenly over the base of a greased 7 x 11-inch cake pan.
2   Place sugar, butter, honey, glucose and condensed milk in a heavy-based saucepan and cook over a low heat, stirring constantly, for 5 minutes or until sugar dissolves. Increase heat to medium and cook, stirring constantly, for 10 minutes or until mixture is a dark red color and starts to leave sides of pan.
3   Pour caramel mixture over fruit and nuts in pan and and leave for 1 hour or until set. Using a cleaver or heavy knife, chop into small pieces and store between sheets of waxed paper in an airtight container.

TUILES

Cook only one tray of tuiles at a time and work quickly when molding, as they set very quickly. If the tuiles set before being molded, return them to the oven for 30 seconds to 1 minute so that they regain their pliability.

Makes 24

- ☐ $1/4$ cup ($1/2$ stick) butter
- ☐ 2 egg whites
- ☐ $1/2$ cup all-purpose flour
- ☐ $1/2$ cup superfine sugar
- ☐ 1 teaspoon vanilla extract
- ☐ $3/4$ cup flaked almonds

1   Preheat the oven to (325°). Line a cookie sheet with nonstick parchment paper. Place butter, egg whites, flour, sugar and vanilla in a food processor or blender and process until smooth.
2   Drop spoonfuls of mixture onto prepared cookie sheet and spread out to make thin circles with $2^1/_2$-inch diameters. Leave 2-inch space between each cookie to allow for spreading. Sprinkle with almonds and bake in the preheated oven for 5-7 minutes or until golden.
3   Stand cookies on sheet for 1 minute, then using a spatula carefully remove from tray, place over a rolling pin and cool.

CHOC-ALMOND FUDGE SQUARES

Makes 25

- ☐ $3/4$ cup superfine sugar
- ☐ 3 tablespoons light molasses
- ☐ $1/2$ cup (1 stick) butter or margarine
- ☐ 1 cup sweetened condensed milk
- ☐ 1 cup plain sweet cookie crumbs
- ☐ 1 cup chopped almonds
- ☐ 7 ounces unsweetened chocolate, chopped

1   Place sugar, molasses, butter and condensed milk in a saucepan and cook over a low heat, stirring constantly, for 5 minutes or until sugar dissolves. Bring to a boil, without stirring, then reduce heat and simmer for 5 minutes.
2   Add cookie crumbs, almonds and chocolate and stir until chocolate melts and mixture is combined. Pour mixture into a greased and lined shallow 7 x 11-inch cake pan and chill until set. Cut into squares.

BUTTERSCOTCH

Makes about 500 g (1 lb)

- ☐ 2 cups firmly packed brown sugar
- ☐ $1/2$ cup honey
- ☐ $1/2$ cup (1 stick) butter or margarine, cut into pieces
- ☐ 1 tablespoon white wine vinegar
- ☐ $1/2$ cup water
- ☐ 2 tablespoons vanilla extract

1   Place sugar, honey, butter, vinegar and water in a large heavy-based saucepan and cook over a medium heat for 10 minutes or until sugar is completely dissolved. Brush sugar crystals sticking to sides of pan frequently with a brush dipped in cold water. Bring to a boil, without stirring, and cook until mixture reaches the hard crack stage 300°F on a sugar thermometer.
2   Stir in vanilla and pour mixture onto a buttered cookie sheet. Set aside to cool, then break into pieces.

CARAMEL CRUNCH

Makes 36 triangles

- ☐ $1^1/_2$ cup plain cookie crumbs
- ☐ $1/2$ cup (1 stick) butter or margarine, melted

CARAMEL CRUNCH FROSTING
- ☐ 1 cup sweetened condensed milk
- ☐ $1/3$ cup light molasses
- ☐ $1/3$ cup butter, chopped
- ☐ $1/2$ cup firmly packed brown sugar
- ☐ $1^1/_2$ cups unsweetened puff rice cereal

1   Place cookie crumbs and butter in a bowl and mix to combine. Press into a greased and lined shallow 7 x 11-inch cake pan and refrigerate until firm.
2   To make frosting, place condensed milk, molasses, butter and sugar in a saucepan and cook, stirring, over a low heat until smooth. Bring to a boil and boil for 5 minutes, stirring constantly. Stir in rice cereal and pour over bottom. Refrigerate until firm, then cut into triangles.

CORNFLAKE CRUNCHIES

Makes 40

- ☐ $1/2$ cup (1 stick) butter or margarine
- ☐ $1/3$ cup light molasses
- ☐ 4 cups cornflakes
- ☐ $1/3$ cup shredded coconut
- ☐ $1/2$ cup chocolate chips
- ☐ $1/2$ cup pecans, chopped

1   Place butter and molasses in a saucepan and cook, stirring, over a low heat until butter melts. Bring to simmering and simmer for 3-4 minutes or until mixture is thick and syrupy.
2   Place cornflakes, coconut, chocolate chips and pecans in a bowl and mix to combine. Pour in molasses mixture and mix well. Place spoonfuls of mixture in paper bake cups and refrigerate until set.

Choc-Almond Fudge Squares, Tuiles

CHOCOLATE CASHEW TOFFEE

Makes 25

- [ ] **2 cups firmly packed brown sugar**
- [ ] **$1/_2$ cup light molasses**
- [ ] **$3/_4$ cup ($1^1/_2$ sticks) butter**
- [ ] **2 tablespoons vinegar**
- [ ] **4 ounces unsweetened chocolate, chopped**
- [ ] **2 tablespoons solid vegetable shortening**
- [ ] **1 cup roasted unsalted cashews, chopped**

1   Place sugar, molasses, butter and vinegar in a saucepan and cook over a medium heat, without boiling, for 5 minutes or until sugar dissolves. Increase heat, bring to a boil and cook, without stirring, until mixture is golden.

2   Remove pan from heat, allow bubbles to subside, then pour mixture into a greased shallow 7 x 11-inch cake pan. Allow to set.

3   Place chocolate and vegetable shortening in a heatproof bowl set over a saucepan of simmering water and cook, stirring, until chocolate and shortening melts and is combined. Spread chocolate mixture evenly over toffee and sprinkle with cashews. Allow to set. Using a heavy knife, cut into pieces.

CHOCOLATE ALMOND SQUARES

Makes about 18

- [ ] **$1^1/_2$ cups slivered almonds, roughly chopped**
- [ ] **$2/_3$ cup all-purpose flour**
- [ ] **2 eggs**
- [ ] **$1/_3$ cup superfine sugar**
- [ ] **$1/_2$ cup light molasses**
- [ ] **$1/_4$ cup ($1/_2$ stick) butter, melted**
- [ ] **5 ounces milk chocolate, melted**

CHOCOLATE FROSTING
- [ ] **5 ounces unsweetened chocolate, melted**
- [ ] **3 tablespoons melted butter**

1   Preheat the oven to moderate (350°). Grease and line a 10-inch square cake pan.

2   Place almonds and flour in a bowl, mix to combine and set aside.

3   Place eggs and sugar in a separate bowl and beat until thick and creamy. Beat in molasses, butter and chocolate, then stir into almond mixture.

4   Pour mixture into the prepared cake pan and bake in preheated moderate oven (350°) for 30 minutes. Turn onto a wire rack to cool.

5   For frosting, place melted chocolate and melted butter in a bowl mix to combine. Spread frosting over cooked layer and allow to set, then cut into squares.

CHOCOLATE CRACKLES

Makes 12

- [ ] **2 cups unsweetened puffed rice cereal**
- [ ] **$3/_4$ cup IOX (confectioners') sugar, sifted**
- [ ] **1 tablespoon unsweetened cocoa powder, sifted**
- [ ] **$1/_2$ cup flaked coconut**
- [ ] **$1/_2$ cup solid vegetable shortening, melted and cooled**

1   Place rice cereal, IOX (confectioners') sugar, cocoa powder and coconut in a bowl and mix to combine.

2   Pour in shortening and mix well. Place spoonfuls of mixture in paper bake cups and allow to set.

Chocolate Cashew Toffee

WALNUT CRUNCHIES

Makes about 18

- ☐ $\frac{1}{2}$ cup (1 stick) butter
- ☐ $\frac{2}{3}$ cup granulated brown (raw or demerara) sugar
- ☐ 2 tablespoons light molasses
- ☐ 1 egg, lightly beaten
- ☐ 1 cup flaked coconut
- ☐ $1\frac{3}{4}$ cup wholewheat flour
- ☐ $1\frac{1}{2}$ teaspoons baking powder
- ☐ 1 cup walnuts halves

1　Preheat the oven to (300°). Lightly grease cookie sheets.

2　Melt butter in a saucepan over a low heat. Stir in sugar, molasses and egg. Add coconut, flour and baking powder and mix to combine.

2　Take teaspoons of mixture and roll into small balls. Place balls $1\frac{1}{4}$-inch apart on cookie sheets. Press a walnut half into the top of each ball, flatten cookies slightly and bake in the preheated oven (300°) for 30 minutes or until golden. Cool cookies on wire racks.

SESAME CARAMELS

Makes about 60

- ☐ 1 cup sesame seeds
- ☐ 1 cup firmly packed brown sugar
- ☐ $\frac{1}{3}$ cup butter
- ☐ 2 tablespoons honey
- ☐ $\frac{1}{3}$ cup liquid glucose
- ☐ $\frac{1}{2}$ cup sweetened condensed milk
- ☐ $\frac{1}{4}$ cup sunflower seeds, chopped

1　Place sesame seeds in skillet and cook over a low heat, stirring constantly, for 4-5 minutes or until seeds are golden. Remove seeds from skillet and cool.

2　Place sugar, butter, honey, glucose and condensed milk in a large saucepan and cook over a low heat, stirring constantly and without boiling, for 5 minutes or until sugar dissolves. Slowly bring to a boil and cook, stirring constantly, for 7 minutes.

3　Stir sunflower seeds and $\frac{1}{4}$ cup toasted sesame seeds into caramel mixture and mix well to combine. Pour mixture into an aluminum foil-lined 7x 11 x $1\frac{1}{2}$-inch cake pan and set aside to cool to room temperature.

4　Cut caramel into 4 strips lengthwise, fold each strip in half and roll into a log with a $\frac{3}{4}$-inch diameter. Roll logs in remaining sesame seeds and refrigerate until firm. Cut into slices.

CHOCOLATE NUT WREATHS

Makes 10-12

- ☐ 7 ounces unsweetened chocolate, melted
- ☐ $\frac{1}{2}$ cup slivered almonds, roughly chopped
- ☐ $\frac{1}{2}$ cup chopped glacé cherries, red, green and yellow

Grease and line a tray with nonstick parchment paper. Using a teaspoon, spoon a little melted chocolate onto parchment paper and spread out to form a wreath shape. Decorate with almonds and glacé cherries and refrigerate until firm. Repeat with remaining chocolate, almonds and cherries to use all ingredients.

Sesame Caramels

Gourmet delicacies

The gourmet food booth offers buyers all the fine produce of a country garden and gourmet restaurant combined — fruity marmalades and jams, delicate herbed vinegars, spicy pickles and relishes, pork pies and pâtés.

Preparations for your gourmet booth should begin as early as possible with the collection of an interesting selection of bottles, jars and crocks. Use medium-sized jars for jams and chutneys and small jars and crocks for mustard. Old vinegar and wine bottles are great for herb vinegars (see page 39). Use clear glass whenever possible; colored glass detracts from the appeal of the contents.

Ask your team of volunteer gourmet cooks for their specialities to add to your list of goods to make. Once you have decided what to include in your booth, divide your products into categories, such as relishes and chutneys, pastes and pâtés, and prepare a master plan for each group including:

❖ recipes and ingredients
❖ instructions for bottling and packaging
❖ method of storage until delivery
❖ special tips such as those for jam making

Give each gourmet cook a copy of the master plan with the recipes and quantities he or she has agreed to make clearly marked.

Collect the goods at least a day or two before the big day to add any final touches to the packaging. Cover tops of jars with pretty floral or gingham fabrics. Even small paper doilies can look wonderful. Tie them in place with ribbon or cord. Make decorative labels for all your products, attach a sprig of herbs or dried flowers to the tags. Prepare bouquets garnis (see page 39) in squares of cheesecloth, gathered and tied with colorfast embroidery floss. Delicious pork pies can be attractively boxed in batches of six, or wrapped individually in cellophane.

PRICES

Aim to offer a range of products at various prices, keeping them under local retail prices whenever possible. If you have kept your costs down, you will be able to sell at very reasonable prices and still make excellent profits.

DECORATION

Decorate the booth in "gourmet" colors like terra cotta and dark green. Use baskets filled with fresh fruit or vegetables or herbs growing in clay pots to add to the pleasant country atmosphere.

When displaying your goods, make the most of their mouth-watering appearance. Arrange brandied apricots beside mint jelly and lemon butter beside plum jam. Place small jars at the front of the stand and larger bottles at the rear. Use baskets or terra cotta bowls to

present bouquets garnis and other herbs (see page 39). Keep pâtés or pork pies well chilled, only displaying a few at a time and replenishing stock frequently.

❖ PICKLED ONIONS ❖

Makes about 4 pints

- ☐ **4 pounds pearl or small white onions**
- ☐ **¹/₂ cup coarse (Kosher) cooking salt**
- ☐ **5 cups distilled white vinegar**
- ☐ **1 tablespoon sugar**
- ☐ **1¹/₂ teaspoons whole cloves**
- ☐ **2 teaspoons whole allspice**
- ☐ **2 teaspoons whole black peppercorns**
- ☐ **2 bay leaves**

1 Cover unpeeled onions with boiling water and stand for 2 minutes. Drain and plunge into cold water. Peel onions and combine with salt in a large nonmetal bowl. Pour over enough cold water to just cover onions, cover and refrigerate.
2 Place vinegar and sugar in a medium saucepan and bring to a boil.
3 Combine cloves, allspice, peppercorns, bay leaves and cloves in several layers of cheesecloth. Tie together to form a bag and drop into boiling vinegar mixture. Cook for 5 minutes, then remove pan from heat and cool mixture 2 to 3

CANNING INSTRUCTIONS

1 Wash pint-sized canning jars, lids and bands in hot soapy water. Rinse. Leave jars in hot water until needed. Place the lids and bands in a saucepan of simmering water until ready to use.
2 When filling the clean, hot canning jars leave a ¹/₄-inch headspace.
3 Run a long, thin nonmetallic spatula around the inside of the jars to release trapped air bubbles. Wipe the jar rims and threads clean with a damp cloth. Cover the jars with the hot lids; screw on the bands firmly.
4 When processing the jars in a boiling water bath the water should cover the jars by 1 or 2 inches.
5 Remove the jars from the boiling water to a wire rack. Let stand for 12 hours. Test for seals. Label, date and store in a cool, dark place.

COOK'S TIP

Brandied apricots are best stored in a cool, dark place. For full flavor to develop, store for one month before using.

COOK'S TIP

Use clean unchipped jars. Remove any labels. Cold glass will crack if heat is suddenly applied.

hours at room temperature. Remove and discard spice bag.

4   Wash four pint-sized canning jars (see Step 1 - Canning Instructions page 26).

5   Drain onions and rinse under cold running water.

6   Using clean, sterilized tongs, pack firmly into the clean, hot canning jars. Make sure there is enough liquid to cover the onions; if necessary, add additional vinegar. (See Steps 2 to 3 - Canning Instructions page 26.)

7   Process the jars for 10 minutes (see Steps 4 to 5 Canning Instructions page 26).

❖ BRANDIED APRICOTS ❖

Makes about 3 half-pint jars

- ☐ **2 cups sugar**
- ☐ **1 cup water**
- ☐ **2¹/₂ pounds apricots, peeled, halved and pitted**

- ☐ **¹/₄ teaspoon ground nutmeg**
- ☐ **1 cup brandy**

1   Wash three half-pint canning jars (see Step 1 - Canning Instructions page 26).

2   Combine sugar and water in a large enameled or stainless steel saucepan. Cook over medium heat, stirring until sugar dissolves. Add apricots and nutmeg, simmering for 4 to 6 minutes or until apricots are just tender.

3   Remove apricots with a slotted spoon and pack tightly into the sterilized, clean, hot canning jars. Bring syrup to the boil and continue boiling for about 8 minutes or until reduced by half and light golden brown. Make sure there is enough liquid to cover the apricots; if necessary, mix equal quantities of syrup and brandy. (See Steps 2 to 3 - Canning Instructions page 26.)

4   Process the jars in a boiling water bath for 15 minutes (see Steps 4 to 5 - Canning Instructions page 26).

Beautifully packaged gourmet delicacies

❖ BREAD AND BUTTER ❖
CUCUMBERS

Makes about 4 pint jars

- ☐ **2¹/₂ pounds (about 15) Kirby cucumbers, sliced (about 8 cups)**
- ☐ **2 large onions, sliced (2 cups)**
- ☐ **1 medium sweet green pepper, cored, seeded and cut into thin slices**
- ☐ **¹/₃ cup coarse (Kosher) salt**
- ☐ **water**
- ☐ **2¹/₂ cups distilled white vinegar**
- ☐ **1¹/₂ cups sugar**
- ☐ **2 teaspoons mustard seeds**
- ☐ **1 teaspoon celery seeds**
- ☐ **1 teaspoon whole all spice**

1   Combine cucumbers, onions and green pepper in a large enameled or stainless steel dish. Sprinkle with salt and pour over enough water to cover vegetables. Stand for 5 hours, then drain and rinse over cold running water.

2   Wash 4 pint-size canning jars (see Step 1 - Canning Instructions page 26).

3   Place vinegar, sugar, mustard seeds, celery seeds and mixed spice in a large enameled or stainless steel saucepan and cook over low heat, stirring until sugar dissolves. Add vegetables and bring to a boil over medium heat. Remove from heat.

4   Using clean, sterilized tongs, pack vegetables tightly into hot sterilised jars. Make sure there is enough liquid to cover the vegetables; if necesary, add additional vinegar. (See Steps 2 to 3 - Canning Instructions page 26.)

5   Process the jars in a boiling water bath for 10 minutes (see Steps 4 to 5 - Canning Instructions page 26).

❖ TOMATO RELISH ❖

Store relishes in a cool, dark place. The flavour improves if left for three to four weeks before using.

Makes 3 pint jar

- [ ] **3¹/₂ pounds tomatoes, peeled and chopped**
- [ ] **¹/₂ cup coarse (Kosher) salt**
- [ ] **4 onions, chopped (4 cups)**
- [ ] **2¹/₂ cups distilled white vinegar**
- [ ] **1³/₄ cups sugar**
- [ ] **4-5 small red chili peppers, seeded and finely chopped**
- [ ] **1 tablespoon curry powder**
- [ ] **1 tablespoon ground turmeric**
- [ ] **2 teaspoons prepared hot mustard**
- [ ] **1 teaspoon ground cumin**
- [ ] **2 tablespoons all-purpose flour**
- [ ] **water**

1   Place tomatoes in a large glass bowl, sprinkle with salt, cover, and let stand overnight.

2   Drain tomatoes and rinse under cold running water, then combine with onions and vinegar in a large saucepan. Bring to the boil, reduce heat and simmer for 10 minutes. Add sugar and chili peppers, stir until sugar is dissolved and simmer 5 minutes.

3   Combine curry powder, turmeric, mustard, cumin, and flour in a small bowl with enough cold water to make a paste. Whisk into the simmering tomato mixture and cook for 1 hour over low heat, or until mixture thickens, stirring from time to time.

4   Wash 3 pint-sized canning jars (see Step 1 - Canning Instructions page 26).

5   Pack the relish into the clean, hot canning jars, using a wide-mouth funnel. Make sure there is enough liquid to cover the relish; if necesary, add additional vinegar. (See Steps 2 to 3 - Canning Instructions page 26.)

6   Process the jars in a boiling water bath for 15 minutes (see Steps 4 to 5 - Canning Instructions page 26).

❖ SPICY APPLE CHUTNEY ❖

Makes about 2 pint jars

- [ ] **2 tablespoons vegetable oil**
- [ ] **1 clove garlic, crushed**
- [ ] **1 teaspoon grated fresh ginger**
- [ ] **2 fresh green chili peppers, seeded and chopped**
- [ ] **2 tablespoons mustard seeds**
- [ ] **1 teaspoon pumpkin pie spice**
- [ ] **15 whole black peppercorns**
- [ ] **2 teaspoons ground cumin**
- [ ] **1 teaspoon ground allspice**
- [ ] **1 teaspoon ground turmeric**
- [ ] **8 large cooking apples, peeled, cored and sliced**
- [ ] **²/₃ cup distilled white vinegar**
- [ ] **¹/₂ cup sugar**

1   Heat oil in a large saucepan over medium heat. Add garlic, ginger and chili peppers and cook, stirring occasionally, for 2 to 3 minutes. Combine mustard seeds, pumpkin pie spice, peppercorns, cumin, allspice and turmeric in a small bowl. Add to garlic mixture and cook, stirring occasionally, for 3 to 4 minutes.

2   Add apples, vinegar and sugar and bring to boil over medium heat. Reduce heat to low and simmer, stirring occasionally, for about 1 hour or until thickened.

3   Meanwhile, wash two pint-size canning jars (see Step 1 - Canning Instructions page 26.)

4   Pack the chutney into the clean, hot canning jars, using a wide-mouth funnel. Make sure there is enough liquid to cover the chutney; if necesary, add additional vinegar. (See Steps 2 to 3 - Canning Instructions page 26.)

5   Process the jars in a boiling water bath for 5 minutes (see Steps 4 to 5 - Canning Instructions page 26).

❖ PLUM JAM ❖

Makes about 3 pint jars

- [ ] **2 pounds damson plums, halved and pitted**
- [ ] **1 cup water**
- [ ] **2 pounds sugar**

1   Wash 3 pint-size canning jars (see Step 1 - Canning Instructions page 26).

2   Combine plums and water in a large heavy metal saucepan. Bring to a boil over high heat; reduce heat to low, cover and simmer for 15 to 20 minutes or until fruit is tender. Add sugar, stirring until the sugar dissolves.

3   Increase heat to medium high; bring to a boil and boil, stirring occasionally, 20 to 30 minutes or until temperature reaches 218° to 222°F on a candy thermometer. Skim foam from surface.
4   Pour the jam into the clean hot canning jars using a wide-mouth funnel (see Steps 2 to 3 - Canning Instructions page 26).
5   Process the jars for 5 minutes (see Steps 4 to 5 - Canning Instructions page 26).

❖ THREE FRUIT ❖ MARMALADE

Makes about 7 half-pint jars

- [ ] **2 large oranges**
- [ ] **2 limes**
- [ ] **1 large grapefruit**
- [ ] **1 quart water**
- [ ] **7 cups sugar**

1   Cut unpeeled fruit in half, then slice thinly and discard seeds. Place fruit in a large nonmetallic bowl and pour over water. Cover and let stand overnight.
2   Meanwhile, wash 7 half-pint canning jars (see Step 1 - Canning Instructions page 26).
3   Transfer fruit and water to a large enameled or stainless steel saucepan. Bring to a boil over high heat; reduce heat to low; simmer for about 1 hour or until fruit is tender. Add sugar, stirring until the sugar dissolves. Increase heat to medium-high, bring to a boil, stirring occasionally for about 45 minutes or until temperature reaches 218° to 222°F on a candy thermometer. Test if marmalade is set. Remove from heat and let stand for 1 to 2 minutes. Skim foam off surface.
4   Pour the marmalade into the clean, hot canning jars (see Steps 2 to 3 - Canning Instructions page 26).
5   Process the jars in a boiling water bath for 5 minutes (see Step 4 to 5 - Canning Instructions page 26).

❖ FIG JAM ❖

Pour warm water over the figs and let set overnight.

Makes about 7 half-pint jars

- [ ] **3¹/₂ pounds dried figs**
- [ ] **1 cup water**
- [ ] **1 tablespoon sugar**

1   Wash 6 half-pint canning jars (see Step 1 - Canning Instructions page 26).
2   Meanwhile, remove the stems from figs and finely chop. Combine figs and water in a large saucepot. Bring to a boil over high heat. Reduce heat to low, simmer for about 15 to 20 minutes or until figs are tender. Add sugar, stirring constantly until sugar dissolves. Increase heat to medium-high, bring to a boil and boil, stirring occasionally 40 to 50 minutes or until temperature reaches 218° to 222°F on a candy thermometer. Test if jam is set. Remove from heat and let stand 1 to 2 minutes. Skim off foam.
4   Pour the jam into the clean, hot canning jars, using a wide-mouth funnel. (See Steps 2 to 3 - Canning Instructions page 26.)
5   Process the jars in a boiling water bath for 5 minutes (see Steps 4 to 5 - Canning Instructions page 26).

❖ LEMON BUTTER ❖

Lemon butter, sometimes called lemon curd, is sure to be a family favorite.

Makes 1 half-pint jar

- [ ] **2 eggs**
- [ ] **¹/₂ cup sugar**
- [ ] **grated rind and juice 2 lemons**
- [ ] **2 tablespoons butter or margarine**

1   Beat eggs and sugar slightly in the top of a double boiler or a small bowl. Add lemon rind and juice and butter. Sit top over a saucepan of simmering water. Cook stirring occasionally for 15 minutes, or until mixture thickens.

2   Meanwhile, wash 1 half-pint canning jar (see Step 1 - Canning Instructions page 26).
3   Spoon mixture into the clean hot canning jar (see Step 2 Canning - Instructions page 26). Cover the jar with the hot lid, screw on lid firmly. Seal and cool to room temperature. Store in the refrigerator.

❖ HORSERADISH MUSTARD ❖

The flavour of this mustard will develop if stored for two to three weeks before using.

Makes about ¹/₂ cup

- [ ] **3 tablespoons dry mustard**
- [ ] **1 tablespoon horseradish**
- [ ] **1 teaspoon salt**
- [ ] **3 tablespoons white wine vinegar**
- [ ] **1 tablespoon olive oil**

1   Combine mustard, horseradish, salt, vinegar and oil in a bowl and blend together. Pour in a small jar with a tight fitting lid. Seal and store in the refrigerator.

❖ APRICOT JAM ❖

Makes about 5 half-pint jars
- [ ] **1 pound dried apricots**
- [ ] **5 cups water**
- [ ] **2 pounds sugar**
- [ ] **almond extract**

1   Combine apricots and water in a large bowl. Cover and stand overnight.
2   Transfer apricots and water to a large enameled or stainless steel saucepan. Bring to a boil over medium heat and cook for 10 minutes or until apricots are tender. Add sugar, stirring constantly until the sugar dissolves. Reduce heat to low and simmer, stirring occasionally, 1 hour or until temperature reaches 218° to 222°F on a candy thermometer. Test if jam is set. Remove from heat and let stand 1 to 2 minutes. Skim off foam.
3   Meanwhile, wash 5 half-pint canning jars (see Step 1 - Canning Instructions page 26).
4   Pour the jam into the clean, hot canning jars, using a wide-mouth funnel (see Steps 2 to 3 - Canning Instructions page 26).
5   Process the jars in a boiling water bath for 5 minutes (see Steps 4 to 5 - Canning

❖ PORK PIES ❖

Makes 6 pies
PASTRY
- ☐ **4 cups unsifted all-purpose flour,**
- ☐ **2 teaspoons salt (1¹/₂ teaspoons if using salted butter or margarine)**
- ☐ **1¹/₂ cups vegetable shortening or unsalted butter or margarine, cut into ¹/₂-inch slices**
- ☐ **¹/₂ cup cold water**
- ☐ **1 egg, lightly beaten**
FILLING
- ☐ **1 pound lean ground pork**
- ☐ **1 cup fresh breadcrumbs**
- ☐ **1 small onion, grated**
- ☐ **1 egg, beaten**
- ☐ **2 tablespoons milk**
- ☐ **¹/₂ teaspoon ground coriander**
- ☐ **¹/₄ teaspoon ground nutmeg**
- ☐ **¹/₂ teaspoon ground thyme**
- ☐ **¹/₄ teaspoon ground sage**

1 Prepare the Pastry: Combine the flour and salt in a large bowl. Cut in half of the shortening, butter or margarine with a pastry blender or 2 knives until the mixture resembles fine meal. Cut in the remaining shortening, butter or margarine until the largest pieces are the size of peas. Gradually add the water, stirring with a fork until the dough leaves the sides of the bowl clean and can be gathered into a ball. Wrap the ball of dough in plastic wrap. Refrigerate for at least 30 minutes before rolling.

2 Grease six 3 x 1³/₄-inch ramekins.

3 Prepare the Filling: Combine pork, breadcrumbs, onion, egg, milk, coriander, nutmeg, thyme and sage in a medium-size bowl. Cover and refrigerate while preparing the pastry.

4 Divide pastry into 2 portions, 1 portion two-thirds larger than the other. Divide the larger portion of pastry into 6 equal portions. Keep all the portions wrapped in plastic wrap and refrigerated except the one that is being rolled. Roll out one piece of pastry on a lightly floured surface to a ¹/₈- inch thickness. Cut to a 6-inch circle using a 6-inch saucer as a guide. Line a prepared ramekin with pastry. Repeat with remaining five portions.

5 Spoon equal amounts of filling into each pastry-lined ramekin.

6 Repeat Step 4 with the smaller piece of dough, cutting each individual portion to a 3-inch circle.

7 Preheat the oven to hot (400°).

8 Moisten the pastry edges of the filled ramekins with water. Fit the 3-inch pastry circles over the filling. Trim the overhang to 1 inch if necessary; fold under to make a stand-up edge; flute. Cut decorative designs or vents in the top for steam to escape. Brush the tops with the beaten egg.

Pork Pies
Cut 6-inch circles.
Crimp edges of pastry to seal.

Chicken Liver Pâté, Salmon Pâté

9 Bake in the preheated hot oven for 40 minutes or until golden brown.(If crust begins to get too dark, cover with foil).

❖ CHICKEN LIVER PATE ❖

Makes 3 to 4 one cup pâtés
- ☐ **1 pound chicken livers, chopped**
- ☐ **4 tablespoons dry sherry**
- ☐ **¹/₂ cup (1 stick) butter or margarine, divided**
- ☐ **2 shallots, finely chopped**
- ☐ **1 clove garlic, crushed**
- ☐ **¹/₄ cup heavy cream**
- ☐ **¹/₂ teaspoon ground thyme**
- ☐ **¹/₄ teaspoon allspice**
- ☐ **salt and pepper to taste**

1 Place livers in a bowl. Cover with sherry and stand for 2 hours. Drain and reserve liquid.

2 Melt 2 tablespoons of the butter in a large (10-inch) skillet over medium heat until bubbly. Add livers, shallots, garlic and cook, stirring occasionally for 3 minutes or until livers lose their pink color. Pour in reserved liquid and cook for 1 minute more. Remove pan from heat.

3 Melt remaining butter and measure 2 tablespoons into the container of an electric food processor or blender. Add the liver mixture, cream and thyme and whirl at high speed until puréed. Season to taste with salt and pepper. Spoon mixture into 1 cup ramekins or custard cups. Pour remaining melted butter over surfaces.

❖ SALMON PATE ❖

Makes 3 to 4 one cup pâtés
- ☐ **1 can (6¹/₂ ounces) red salmon, drained**
- ☐ **¹/₂ cup ricotta cheese**
- ☐ **¹/₂ cup mayonnaise**
- ☐ **2 teaspoons grated lemon rind**
- ☐ **2 tablespoons lemon juice**
- ☐ **3 green onions**
- ☐ **¹/₂ cup (1 stick) butter or margarine, melted**

1 Combine salmon, cheese, mayonnaise, lemon rind and juice, green onions and butter in a food processor or blender. Whirl at high speed until smooth.

2 Spoon mixture into 1 cup ramekins or custard cups. Cover and refrigerate overnight.

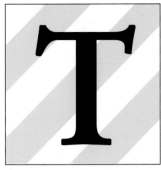# Take-along treats

Working up an appetite is easy! Make sure no one goes hungry with these tempting ideas for the refreshment area or for eating on the go. Package some for take-home, too!

❖ SCONES ❖

Makes 24

- ☐ **4 cups self-rising flour, sifted**
- ☐ **2 tablespoons IOX (confectioners') sugar**
- ☐ **2¹/₂ tablespoons butter or margarine**
- ☐ **1¹/₂ cups milk**

1 Preheat the oven to hot (425°). Grease 2 large baking sheets; set aside.

2 Stir together flour and IOX (confectioners') sugar in a large mixing bowl. Cut in butter with a pastry blender or 2 knives until mixture resembles fine crumbs. Slowly stirring with a fork, add just enough of the milk until the dough is soft and sticky. Do not overmix.

3 Turn dough out onto a lightly floured surface. Knead lightly with floured hands just until smooth. Roll out the dough to a 1-inch thickness. With a 2-inch round cookie cutter, cut out as many scones as possible. Carefully transfer to the prepared baking sheet, spacing 2-inches apart. Re-roll the scraps of dough and cut out as many scones as possible. Brush the tops lightly with milk.

4 Bake in the preheated hot (425°) oven for 12 to 15 minutes, or until the scones are golden. Remove with a spatula to a wire rack.

VARIATIONS

RAISIN SCONES — Add 1 cup raisins to dry ingredients before adding the milk.

DATE SCONES — Add ¹/₂ cup finely chopped dates to dry ingredients before adding the milk.

COOK'S TIP
THE PERFECT SCONE

1 Scone dough should be soft and sticky, turned out onto a lightly floured surface and kneaded quickly and lightly then pressed out with fingertips.

2 A rolling pin is useful for large quantities of dough. Don't roll too thick or too thin – ³/₄-inch is a good thickness.

3 Sugar takes away the dough's floury taste .

4 Add most of the liquid at once and mix only until ingredients are combined. Overmixing will result in heavy, tough scones.

5 Sharp, hollow, metal cookie cutters are best for scones. Flour the cutters and press straight down into dough. Twisting the cutters causes the sides of the scones to drag and inhibits rising.

6 Scones may also be baked using a cake pan with 2-inch high sides rather than on a baking sheet. The sides of the cake pan prevent the scones from falling off the pan. Place scones in the greased pan with sides just touching. Overcrowding will prevent the scones in the middle from cooking evenly.

7 Scones should be cooked at a very high temperature in the middle of the oven. To test for doneness, tap with fingers. They should sound hollow and look evenly browned.

8 Turn out scones onto a wire rack to cool.

9 To freeze scones, cool completely. Place in a freezer bag. Press out excess air and seal. Scones can be frozen for up to two months.

10 Reheat frozen scones in the microwave oven on HIGH (100%) for 1-2 minutes per scone or wrap scones in aluminium foil and warm through in a preheated low oven (300°F).

❖ FRUIT AND NUT ROLLS ❖

Use three washed and dried 10 ³/₄-ounce soup cans with both ends removed to bake these breads. Cover the ends with aluminum foil.

Makes three 6-inch breads

- ☐ ²/₃ **cup chopped mixed dried fruit**
- ☐ **hot water**
- ☐ ¹/₂ **cup (1 stick) butter or margarine, softened**
- ☐ ¹/₂ **cup firmly packed light brown sugar**
- ☐ **3 tablespoons honey**
- ☐ **2 eggs**
- ☐ **1 cup self-rising flour, sifted**
- ☐ ³/₄ **cup all-purpose flour, sifted**
- ☐ ¹/₄ **cup milk**
- ☐ ¹/₂ **cup chopped walnuts**

1 Preheat the oven to moderate (350°). Grease three empty and cleaned 10 ³/₄-ounce soup cans; set aside.
2 Cover fruit with hot water and let stand for 30 minutes. Drain and dry fruit on paper toweling.
3 Cream butter, sugar and honey in a medium-size mixing bowl until light and fluffy. Beat in eggs. Combine flours on a sheet of waxed paper and fold in alternately with the milk, beginning and ending with the flour. Stir in fruit and walnuts.
4 Spoon mixture evenly into three prepared cans. Cover ends with foil and bake in the preheated moderate (350°)

oven for 1 hour. Let breads cool in cans on wire rack for 10 minutes. Turn out of cans onto a wire rack to cool completely.

❖ STRAWBERRY JAM ❖

To test if jam is set, scoop up a small amount of the hot mixture onto a cold metal spoon, cool slightly, tilt. The jam is done when drops of the mixture cling together forming a jam-like sheet, if not set sufficiently, return to the heat, boil a few minutes more and retest for set.

Makes about two half-pint jars

- ☐ **2 pounds strawberries, hulled**
- ☐ **2 pounds sugar**
- ☐ ¹/₂ **cup lemon juice**
- ☐ ³/₄ **cup water**

1 Wash 6 half-pint canning jars (see Step 1 - Canning Instructions page 26).
2 Combine strawberries, sugar, lemon juice and water in a large, heavy saucepan. Cook over low heat, stirring until sugar dissolves.
3 Increase heat to medium-high; bring to a boil and boil, stirring occasionally, 20 to 25 minutes or until the temperature reaches 218°F to 222°F on a candy thermometer. Test to see if the jam is set. Remove from heat and let stand 1 to 2 minutes. Skim foam from surface.
4 Pour the jam into the clean hot canning jars using a wide-mouth funnel (see Steps 2 to 3 - Canning Instructions page 26).

5 Process the jars for 5 minutes (see Steps 4 to 5 - Canning Instuctions page 26).

❖ BLUEBERRY AND APPLE ❖ MUFFINS

Makes 12

- ☐ **3 cups self-rising flour, sifted**
- ☐ ¹/₂ **cup sugar**
- ☐ ¹/₂ **cup butter or margarine**
- ☐ **2 eggs**
- ☐ ¹/₂ **cup milk**
- ☐ ¹/₂ **cup canned sliced apples**
- ☐ ¹/₂ **cup canned blueberries, drained**

1 Preheat the oven to hot (425°). Grease 2¹/₂-inch muffin-pan cups, set aside.
2 Combine the flour and sugar in a large bowl. Cut the butter into the flour mixture with a pastry blender or two knives until crumbly. Beat the eggs and milk in a small bowl. Stir into the flour mixture with a fork, just until the dry ingredients are moistened. Stir in the apples and blueberries. The batter will look lumpy.
3 Fill each prepared muffin-pan cup about three-quarters full with batter, using a large spoon and rubber spatula.
4 Bake in the preheated hot (425°) oven for 15 to 20 minutes or until a wooden pick inserted in the center comes out clean. Remove the pan to a wire rack. Loosen the muffins with a thin metal spatula and remove from the pan at once. Cool slightly on a wire rack. Serve warm.

❖ CHELSEA BUN

Serves 6

- ☐ 1 quantity Scones recipe (page 42)
- ☐ ¹/₄ cup (¹/₂ stick) butter
- ☐ 4 tablespoons firmly packed brown sugar
- ☐ 1 teaspoon pumpkin pie spice
- ☐ 1 cup mixed dried fruit

SUGAR GLAZE
- ☐ 1 tablespoon water
- ☐ 1 tablespoon sugar
- ☐ 1 teaspoon gelatin

1   Preheat the oven to moderate (350°). Grease a shallow 8-inch round cake pan.
2   Make up scone dough as directed in recipe. Roll out dough on a lightly floured surface to form a 8 x 12-inch rectangle.
3   Place butter, brown sugar and pumpkin pie spice in a bowl and beat until smooth. Spread butter mixture over dough, then sprinkle with fruit. Roll up lengthwise and using a sharp knife cut into eight thick slices. Arrange slices in cake pan and bake in preheated moderate oven (350°) for 25-30 minutes or until golden.
4   To make glaze, place water, sugar and gelatin in a saucepan and cook over a low heat, stirring constantly, until sugar and gelatin dissolve. Brush hot bun with glaze. Serve warm or cold.

❖ MINI RAISIN PANCAKES

To make plain pancakes omit mixed spice and sultanas from this recipe.

Makes 20 pancakes

- ☐ 1 cup all-purpose flour
- ☐ 1 teaspoon baking powder
- ☐ 1 teaspoon pumpkin pie spice
- ☐ ¹/₄ cup superfine sugar
- ☐ 3 tablespoons chopped golden seedless raisins
- ☐ 1 egg, lightly beaten
- ☐ ¹/₂ cup milk
- ☐ ¹/₃ cup whipping cream

1   Sift together flour, baking powder and pumpkin pie spice into a bowl. Stir in sugar and golden seedless raisins, then make a well in center of mixture.
2   Combine egg, milk and cream and gradually stir into dry ingredients. Continue mixing until batter is smooth.
3   Cook dessertspoonfuls of mixture in a heated, greased, heavy-based skillet over a medium heat until bubbles appear on the surface, then turn and cook until golden.

❖ PECAN FRUIT LOAF

Serves 8

- ☐ 1¹/₂ cups mixed dried fruit
- ☐ 1 cup water
- ☐ ¹/₂ cup (1 stick) butter
- ☐ 1¹/₂ cups sugar
- ☐ 1 egg
- ☐ 2 cups all-purpose flour
- ☐ 1¹/₂ teaspoons baking powder
- ☐ 1¹/₄ cups pecans, roughly chopped

1   Preheat the oven to moderate (350°). Grease and line a 9 x 5 x 3-inch loaf pan.
2   Place fruit and water in a large saucepan, bring to a boil and cook for 3 minutes. Remove pan from heat and set aside to cool.
3   Place butter and sugar in a bowl and beat until light and creamy. Add egg and continue to beat until well combined. Sift together flour and baking powder. Mix flour mixture and undrained fruit mixture, alternately, into butter mixture. Fold in pecans.
4   Spoon batter into the prepared loaf pan and bake in preheated moderate oven (350°) for 1¹/₄ hours or until golden. Stand in pan for 5 minutes before turning onto a wire rack to cool.

Mini Sultana Pancakes, Pecan Fruit Loaf, Chelsea Bun

Garden crafts

Pretty plants and sweet-smelling potpourri make this booth a "garden of earthly delight". Customers can't resist the natural beauty of these items – as gifts or for their own home gardens.

To make your plant booth a success, plan early and be sure you have dedicated gardeners and plant lovers on your team from the start. Allow plenty of time for cuttings and divisions to be well-rooted. No one wants to buy a plant that is really a leafy stick with no roots!

It will be easier to achieve a professional presentation if you all plan together. There will also be fewer problems with watering if the pots are evenly filled and potted with similar soil.

Arrange a team meeting well in advance of the fair to discuss what group members have growing or what they can acquire. Decide which of these plants are most suitable and reliable for propagation and make a list of the plants you can expect to have for the fair. Plants in bloom are great for display purposes and very easy to sell. Go for colorful favorites rather than interesting, but peculiar, varieties.

Include potpourri and other scented garden products for variety. They sell quickly and in bunches. Be sure to have a selection of "child-sized" plants or cacti. A plant purchased at your garden booth may be a child's first step into the wonderful world of gardening.

Ask for donations of potting soil, small pots, seedling trays, bulbs, seeds and unwanted plants. Your team will do the planting and repotting.

Arrange a short meeting every month before the fair to distribute materials and discuss the planting program. Two weeks before the fair, have a final meeting to discuss transporting plants, decorations, labeling and pricing. Be sure to include care instructions for each plant!

PRICES

Check local nursery and super-market prices, and price your plants to be a little lower than retail. Prices should be clearly marked. No true gardener can resist a bargain.

DECORATION

Plan for a plant theme and decorate the booth accordingly. When practical, all decorations such as hanging herbs, should also be for sale. The booth should be large enough to have all of the plants for sale at eye level. Don't crowd them. Keep back-up stock out of harm's way.

Everything you need for a successful plant stall

46

Tropical palms and ferns are always popular

POTTED PLANTS

Pots: Never pot plants in old rusty tins or plastic containers with permanent labels such as yogurt or margarine. They look awful. Since most fairs last for only one day, all the plants must be sold by the end of the day. Pretty containers help sales. All used containers should be scrubbed with a brush and a little detergent before being used. This removes any disease and ensures better presentation. Although terra cotta containers have a special charm, neat plastic pots will do the job and are lighter to carry. Be sure there are adequate drainage holes in the pots before filling.

WHAT TO SELL

Tropical plants: Sell ferns, palms, tree ferns, rainforest plants and orchids. Decorate with anything green, such as huge fresh banana leaves, to achieve a luxurious and lush mood. Spray lightly, with water during the day to keep everything fresh.

Spring festival: Sell masses of colorful flowering plants such as azaleas, daisies, flowering bulbs, geraniums, primroses, forget-me-nots, Johnny-jump-ups and violets. Sell cut flowers from brightly colored plastic buckets. The flowers in bloom will provide most of the display. Decorate with branches of dogwood, cherry or other fruit blossoms.

Fragrant plants: Sell jasmine, bulbs in flower, herbs, scented geraniums, lavender, gardenia, heliotrope, lilac, roses and plants with aromatic foliage. Decorate with bunches of lavender and branches of fragrant foliage such as eucalyptus leaves.

Indoor plants: Sell palms, dieffenbachia, figs, cyclamens, philodendrons, aspidistras, coleus, dracaenas, asparagus ferns, African violets, begonias, terrarium gardens and ferns. Decorate with hanging baskets of ivy spider plants, peperomia, grape ivy and Boston fern (also for sale).

Perennials: Sell flowering favorites such as iris, dianthus, lilies, euphorbias, primrose, agapanthus, lavender, daisies, salvias, fuchsias, geraniums and roses. Include grey foliage plants. Decorate with garlands of ivy and bunches of red rosehips.

Herbs: Sell all types of herbs including culinary, medicinal, fragrant and those used for dyeing. Include hard-to-get and collector varieties. Sell compatible herbs in herb baskets. Decorate with hanging bunches of dried herbs tied with ribbon (also for sale).

Rockery: Sell miniature and small-growing plants, including alpines, ground covers, succulents and cacti. Decorate with large paper-mache rocks (the kids can help make these).

Colorful flowering plants are sure sellers

Potting soil: Use only a prepared potting soil. Don't use tired soil from the garden. Make sure the soil in the pots is a reasonably open mixture and remove any grass and other weeds. Top off the soil to within about 1-inch of the container top a few days before the fair.

Watering: Water your plants regularly during growing, and on the day before the fair make sure you give them a good watering. Don't try to transport the plants to the booth, or to sell them, when they're dripping wet. Take a watering can along with you on the day only for emergencies.

Labeling: All plants should be clearly labeled with the botanical name, the common name and the size of the full-grown plant. Buy or make plant stakes with labels and use a waterproof pen for marking.

Garden herbs in classic terra cotta pots

HERB BASKETS

Sell container herbs grouped in baskets. Baskets can be found in a profusion of shapes and sizes. Woven baskets must be lined to retain the soil. Cut filter paper or cheesecloth to the shape of the basket and overlap it to hold the soil while allowing good water drainage. Soil used in baskets must be well-drained and fairly rich. Unlike herbs grown in the open garden, container herbs must draw all their nutrients from the small amount of soil in the basket. When you plant several herbs in one container, choose herbs that require similar amounts of water, sun and soil conditions.

Since most herbs are used in the kitchen, arrange a basket of culinary herbs, such as basil, thyme, chives, coriander, marjoram, parsley, sage or tarragon.

Since mint needs more moisture and is inclined to overwhelm other herbs, a separate basket containing a combination of mints is a good idea.

A herbal tea basket could contain chamomile, lemon balm, valerian, peppermint or lemon verbena .

49

Dried sweet-smelling ingredients create delightful potpourri

GARDENER'S TIPS

Everyone collecting and drying herbs and flowers from their gardens should be aware of the following:

1   Pick only blemish-free petals, flowers, leaves and herbs. Pass over all petals that are rain damaged.
2   Gather only on a fine day, preferably after a spell of dry weather.
3   Do not water the plants the day before harvesting.
4   In areas with dew, pick after the morning dew has dried, but before the sun is high.
5   Rose petals and small whole flowers such as violets should be spread out evenly on racks, shallow boxes or newspaper to dry.
6   Herbs, lavender and aromatic foliage can be tied in small loose bunches and hung to dry.
7   Flowers and herbs are best dried away from strong light and where the air can circulate around them.
8   As soon as the plant material is completely dry, store in separate, labelled glass containers with lids. Pick and dry plants as they come into flower and add newly dried petals to the jars. Store in a dark, dry place.

❖

PERFUMED GARDEN

The secret of successful potpourri, sachet mix and dried herbs for culinary and cosmetic purposes lies in the drying process. All ingredients, except for the essential oils, must be thoroughly and quickly dried so that optimum fragrance and color is retained. Any material that has a hint of moisture should be discarded – it could turn the whole batch moldy. Spices will help the potpourri hold its scent and add a special fragrance to it. Spices must be fresh and coarsely ground as needed.

FIXATIVES

Fixatives are essential to help fix and stabilize the overall perfume for a very long time. The most common fixative is orris root powder which slows the evaporation of the oils. When dried, orris root powder has a delicate violet scent. Other fixatives include gum benzoin, sandalwood and oakmoss. Dried citrus rinds such as orange and lemon peel are also good for fixing a scent. Use only the orange or yellow part of the rind, the white pith turns moldy after a time.

ESSENTIAL OILS

Essential oils enhance the scent of most potpourri and sachet blends, but should be used very sparingly. Add one drop at a time, smelling and blending as you go. Fixatives and essential oils can be obtained from a craft or health food store.

POTPOURRI

Use transparent containers for potpourri to show off its colors. Collect attractive glass jars with lids and plastic boxes of different shapes. If you have a lot of potpourri to package, fill cellophane bags and tie with a ribbon. Specially made pottery potpourri containers with cork stoppers are also popular.

The following recipes are only a guide to different styles of potpourri you can make. Adapt them to the plant material you have available. Ingredients can be doubled for a larger mix, but always be cautious when adding essential oils.

Step by Step

Follow our recipes below for French Country, Citrus or Woodsy Potpourri.
1   Place all dried flowers in a large bowl and add the dry fixatives.
2   Add spices and herbs to further enhance the scent. Toss to mix thoroughly.
3   If you want a stronger scent, you may add an essential oil. The more oil you add, the stronger the scent will be. Use an eye dropper for better distribution.
4   After adding oils, mix the potpourri well with your hands. Pour into a large container and seal. Leave to mature for about six weeks.
5   When the potpourri has aged, transfer it to containers for selling and decorate with colorful pressed flowers and ferns.

❖ FRENCH COUNTRY ❖ POTPOURRI

☐ **4 cups red rose petals**
☐ **1 cup lavender flowers**
☐ **1 cup each rosemary, thyme, sage and marjoram**
☐ **2 tablespoons coriander seeds, lightly crushed**
☐ **$1/_2$ cup dried lemon peel**
☐ **1 cup fixative, (see left)**
☐ **6-8 drops rose oil**
☐ **3-4 drops lavender oil**

1   Follow Step by Step instructions above.
2   When potpourri has aged, toss in dried whole cornflowers, red roses and lavender sprigs for decoration.

❖ CITRUS POTPOURRI ❖

- [ ] **8 cups of a combination of any or all of the following: lemon verbena, lemon thyme, lemon-scented geranium and/or lemongrass**
- [ ] **1 cup mint leaves**
- [ ] **1 cup calendula petals**
- [ ] **¹/₂ cup each orange and lemon peel**
- [ ] **1 cup whole allspice, lightly crushed**
- [ ] **1 cup fixative**
- [ ] **6-8 drops lemon verbena oil**
- [ ] **3-4 drops bergamot oil**

1 Follow Step by Step instructions at left.
2 When potpourri has aged, toss in dried daffodils, nasturtiums or daisies for decoration.

❖ WOODSY POTPOURRI ❖

- [ ] **8 cups aromatic foliage which might include eucalyptus leaves, rosemary, scented geraniums, bay leaves, basil, lavender foliage**
- [ ] **2 cups sandalwood chips, cedar chips or pine shavings**
- [ ] **1 cup cinnamon sticks, broken into chunks**
- [ ] **1 cup whole coriander seeds or juniper berries, lightly bruised**

1 Follow Step by Step instructions at left.
2 When potpourri has aged, toss in small pine cones and seed pods for decoration.

❖ AROMATIC BATH ❖ OILS

If you have a lot of flowers and herbs you can make aromatic bath oils.

- [ ] **light, unscented body oil, or almond oil**

Strongly scented flowers like:
- [ ] **roses**
- [ ] **lavender**

and therapeutic herbs:
- [ ] **rosemary**
- [ ] **lemon verbena**
- [ ] **chamomile**
- [ ] **mint**
- [ ] **thyme**

1 Pour 6 cups of oil into a large bowl. Add as many flowers or herbs as the bowl will hold and saturate the petals or leaves.
2 Soak flowers and herbs in oil for 24 hours.

Gourmet herb vinegars

3 Remove flowers or herbs with slotted spoon and discard. Add more fresh flowers or herbs to oil.
4 Repeat with six batches of flowers or herbs, then strain liquid through cheesecloth.
5 Transfer oil to attractive bottles and cap tightly.

DRIED HERBS
Sell dried herbs in separate cellophane bags for use in the kitchen, and bath. Be sure to provide instructions for use on each package.

Culinary: Those that retain their flavor best when dried include rosemary, thyme, mint, oregano, marjoram, and bay leaves. Wrap several savory dried herbs together in a square of cheesecloth to make a bouquet garni. Sell some at the gourmet foods booth, too.
Herbal teas: Popular herbs for teas include chamomile, lemongrass, peppermint and a rose petal and lemon verbena blend.
Hair rinses: Herbal hair rinses are used as a final rinse after washing hair. Boil a handful of herbs for 20 minutes and strain. Chamomile is best for blonds and rosemary for brunettes.

❖ HERB VINEGARS ❖

Flavored vinegar can give extra flavor to any savory dish, pickle or salad that normally calls for vinegar in the recipe.

- [ ] **distilled white vinegar**

Flavorful herbs like:
- [ ] **rosemary**
- [ ] **thyme**
- [ ] **tarragon**
- [ ] **basil**
- [ ] **mint**
- [ ] **lemongrass**

1 Wash herbs gently, shake and pat dry thoroughly.
2 Combine 2 cups of slightly crushed fresh herb leaves to every quart of vinegar.
3 Pour vinegar over the herbs in a large nonmetallic bowl; seal and leave for about one week.
4 Strain the liquid and discard the herbs.
5 Repeat the process using fresh leaves and leave again for another week.
6 Strain the vinegar into sterilized bottles or jars and insert a whole sprig or two of the herb used into each of the appropriate vinegars. Seal and label.

Packaging & presentation

Attractive packaging can boost your sales and add beauty and excitement to the "big day". Here is a "feast" of practical and fun presentation ideas to make all of your wares irresistible.

Use attractive hang tags to label candies, and wrap them in clear cellophane – it's the best way to tempt a prospective buyer! Remember candies and cakes must be stored at the appropriate temperature. Wrap fudge and rocky road before the big day, but make sure they don't sweat and become moist.

For bouquet garni, keep cheesecloth bags spotlessly clean and use colorfast embroidery floss to tie them. Line some boxes and bowls with pretty print fabric, fill them with the bouquet garni and arrange them around your booth.

Make the most of mouth-watering candy apples by wrapping them in clear cellophane – gather the cellophane around the apple sticks and tie it with pretty ribbons.

For herb vinegars, use bottles of all different shapes and sizes – and seal them with a cork so they really look the part. Place a sprig of the appropriate herb in the bottle for decoration.

Uniformly shaped packages like our sewing cases and covered picture frames are easy to wrap. Set up a production line of volunteers to get it all done in a jiffy! Use generous amounts of clear cellophane to show off items.

Show off the colors and textures of gourmet jams and relishes in plain jars topped with pretty country-style calico and lace covers. Ask a helper with neat handwriting to label each, using stick-on labels – if you can, use decorative labels as we have. Complete the effect with beautiful curling ribbons in complementary colors. Arrange gourmet baskets with a selection of tempting goods. Line each basket with clear cellophane or tissue paper, wind fabric or florist's ribbon around the handle and base. Use one as the centerpiece for the booth.

Collect plain white cake boxes or ones with patterns as we have here. If you like, decorate the boxes yourself using colorful stickers, markers or stamps and a stamp pad. Tie each box with curling ribbons in several colors. If you are using clear cellophane to present your cakes (see page 8), place toothpicks in the cake top to hold the wrapping away from the icing, gather at the top and secure with some ribbon and a hang tag.

Craft creations

No fair or bazaar would be complete without a craft booth, filled with wonderful handmade items from traditional coat hangers and potholders to the decorative fabric-covered picture frames and lovely rose-trimmed hair accessories.

Start planning your craft booth as early as you can. Unlike cakes and candies, craft items can be made many months in advance and stored quite easily. Call a meeting of all those interested in contributing to a craft booth. Members of your team may have special talents, such as stenciling or making lavender sachets and will be happy to make a number of these for the booth, but others will require some inspiration and direction.

Once you know who can do what, draw up a list of items to be made, taking into account all the skills you have at your disposal, and making sure there is a job for everyone who wants to participate. There will be many simple tasks for willing hands!

You will have to make decisions about whether to "buy or beg" the necessary materials for each project. Make lists of all the materials you will need including fabrics, ribbons, lace, baskets, boxes and so on. Contact local merchants for donations, or buy in bulk if you'll receive a discount. Try to supply your crafters with as many "raw" materials as you can.

Make up a master plan and give all the team members a copy with their own projects highlighted. Prepare copies of patterns and instructions, and lists of all materials required and where they can be obtained.

The master plan should also indicate a timetable for the work to be done and a projected collection day. Don't leave the collection to the last minute; unforeseen problems could leave you short of craft items to sell with no time to make up the difference. The schedule should give you plenty of time to check, wrap and price your wares.

Most of us love a little company while we work, and a "sewing day" is a great way to share skills and ideas around the group. Organize several group sewing days and make them preliminary collection days as well.

PRICES

A price should reflect the cost, work and care that has gone into making an item, but still be below the price charged for a similar item in a store. Each item should be clearly priced. Use small hang tags or removable stickers.

DECORATION

Decorated baskets make wonderful containers for small items. Cover the counter with a pretty fabric or some firm paper. Don't crowd the booth. Keep extra items in covered boxes under the counter.

A collection of crafty creations to make

❖ FLOWER PRESS ❖

Average: For those with some experience in woodworking.

- ☐ **two pieces of plywood, each 7-inch square and ³/₄-inch-thick**
- ☐ **four 2-inch long bolts**
- ☐ **four wing nuts and four washers to fit bolts**
- ☐ **corrugated cardboard**
- ☐ **sandpaper**
- ☐ **sheets of blotting paper**
- ☐ **stenciling equipment (see How to Stencil, right)**
- ☐ **off-white paint**
- ☐ **drill, with bit to match diameter of bolt**
- ☐ **paintbrush**

Directions:
1   With sandpaper round off corners of plywood and paint with off-white paint.
2   Make stencil and stencil motif onto one piece of plywood following How to Stencil, right.
3   Mark and drill holes for bolts at each corner of plywood pieces, taking care to align holes in top and bottom pieces.
4   Cut several sheets of cardboard and blotting paper each 7-inch square. Cut off corners to allow for bolts.
5   Insert bolts through bottom, unstenciled piece of plywood. Layer sheets of cardboard and blotting paper on top of plywood. Place stenciled plywood over cardboard, passing bolts through holes.
6   Attach washers and wing nuts.
7   To use press, lay your chosen flowers on blotting paper, cover with another sheet of blotting paper and then a sheet of cardboard. Continue to assemble layers in this fashion. Close the press, tightening nuts, and place in a cool, dry place. Open the press after about three weeks to check progress. If flowers are completely dry and papery to the touch they are ready to be removed from press.

❖ MUSHROOM BAG ❖

Average: For those with some experience in sewing.

- ☐ **stenciling equipment (see How to Stencil, right)**
- ☐ **16 x 20-inch piece of muslin**
- ☐ **1 yard of ¹/₂-inch-wide twill tape**
- ☐ **thread to match fabric**

Directions:
1   Make stencil and stencil motif on front of bag following How to Stencil, at right.
2   Fold muslin in half, with right sides facing and short sides matching. Stitch up two sides with ¹/₄-inch seams, leaving opening at top.
3   Turn in ¹/₄-inch at top raw edge, and then another 2-inches. Stitch a hem across top.
4   Stitch center of tape to one side of bag.

Reinforce by stitching a box shape with an X through it. Knot ends of tape to finish.

❖ SUN HAT ❖

Easy: Achievable by anyone.

- ☐ **wide-brimmed straw hat**
- ☐ **stenciling equipment**

Directions:
1   Make stencil of roses and leaves, following How to Stencil, right.
2   Stencil roses and leaves motif around hat brim using photo as a guide.

❖ FLOWER POTS ❖

Easy: Achievable by anyone.

- ☐ **terra cotta pots**
- ☐ **stenciling equipment (see How to Stencil, right)**
- ☐ **paintbrush**

Directions:
1   Make stencil. Stencil motif around pots.
2   Using stencil paints, decorate pots with bows and small flowers painted freehand.

❖ TEDDY BEAR PILLOW ❖

Average: For those with some experience in sewing.

- ☐ **stenciling equipment (see How to Stencil, right)**
- ☐ **piece of muslin, 17 inches square**
- ☐ **two pieces of backing fabric, each 17 x 9 inches**
- ☐ **16-inch-square pillow form**
- ☐ **3²/₃ yards of 5-inch-wide strips of backing fabric**
- ☐ **3²/₃ yards of 1-inch-wide lace**
- ☐ **two small shirt buttons**
- ☐ **12-inch-long zipper**
- ☐ **thread to match fabric**

Directions:
1   (¹/₄-inch seams allowed). Stitch together backing fabric strips to form a continuous circle. Fold strips in half, wrong sides together. Press. Stitch lace to folded edge. Gather raw edges of ruffle to fit around 16-inch-square pillow.
2   Make stencil and stencil teddy bear motif onto muslin, following How to Stencil.
3   Stitch ruffle around edge of stenciled muslin, right side together and raw edges even.
4   Stitch only lower ends of pillow back center seam. Insert zipper.
5   Place pillow front and back together with right sides facing. Stitch edges through all thicknesses. Turn right side out

Note: See stencil patterns, pages 58-59.

through zipper opening.
6   Stitch two shirt buttons below Teddy's bow tie. Stuff with pillow form.

HOW TO STENCIL

- ☐ **acetate or Mylar® sheet for cutting stencils**
- ☐ **stencil brushes**
- ☐ **stencil paints in colors of your choice**
- ☐ **felt-tipped pen**
- ☐ **utility knife**
- ☐ **bread board or similar cutting surface**
- ☐ **masking tape**

Directions:
1   Tape acetate sheet over stencil design. With felt-tipped pen, trace around the design. Make a separate stencil for each color.
2   On the first stencil, cut out all the motifs to be painted in the first color with the utility knife. On the second stencil, cut out the motifs to be painted in the second color. Repeat until you have one stencil cut for each color. The uncut outlines will help you center the stencils as you paint each layer.
3   Decide where you want your motif to fall and place the largest piece first.
4   Painting with flat surface of brush, carefully fill in color, using light dabbing motions rather than strokes. Do not use too much paint and use a separate brush for each color. Practice stenciling on scraps until pleased with your results.
5   Stencil each design element until motif is complete.
6   Wash stencils thoroughly after use. Stencils may be reused.

Inset: Mushroom bag keeps mushrooms fresh in the fridge

Stenciling adds a finishing touch to ready-made items

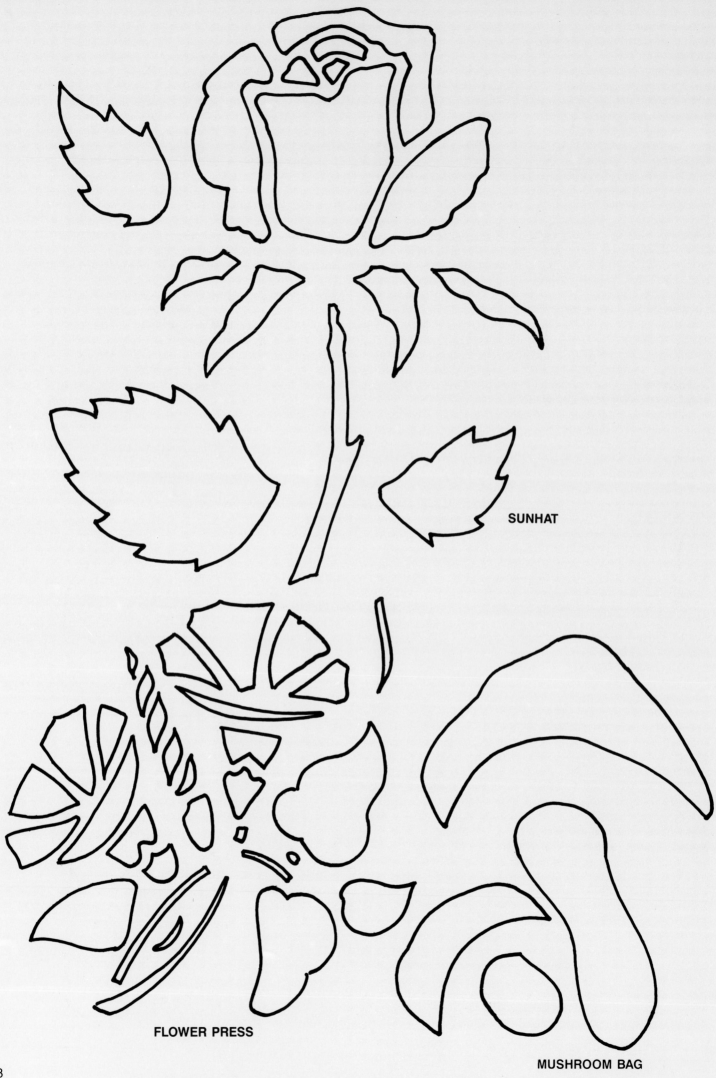

SUNHAT

FLOWER PRESS

MUSHROOM BAG

58

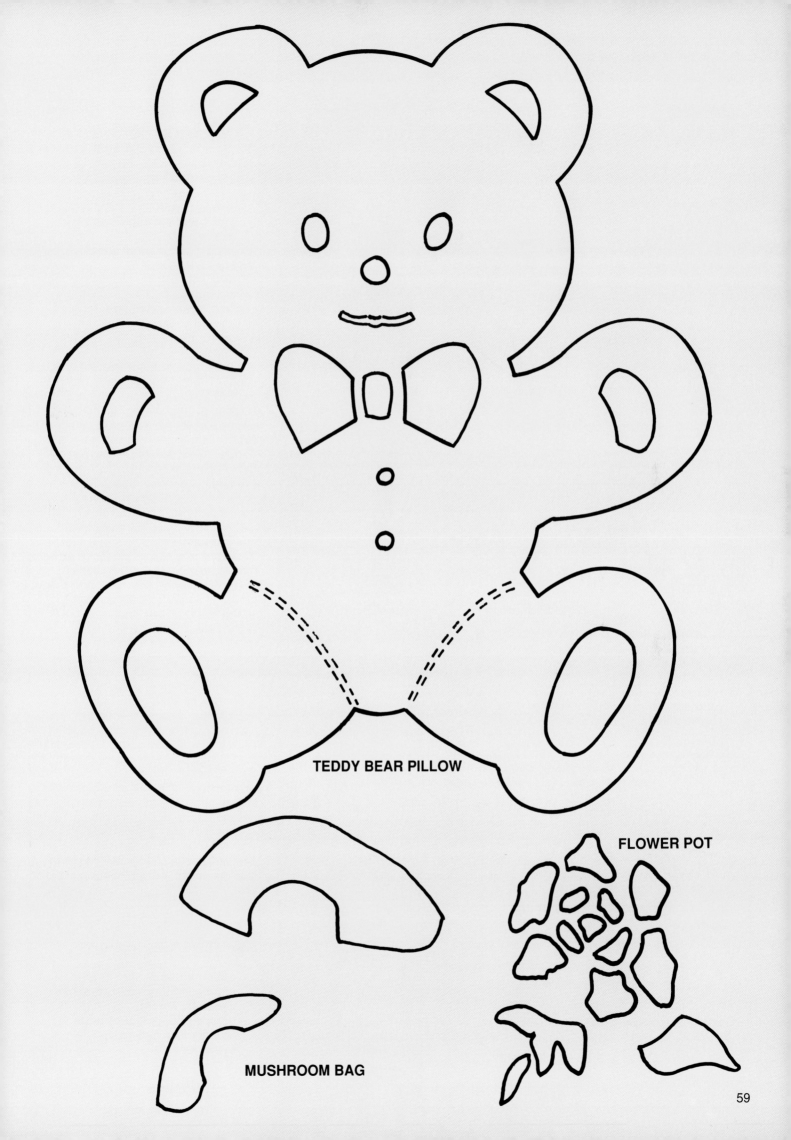

TEDDY BEAR PILLOW

FLOWER POT

MUSHROOM BAG

❖ FABRIC-COVERED ❖ PICTURE FRAMES

Easy: Achievable by anyone

- ☐ **strong cardboard in desired size**
- ☐ **fabric and synthetic batting in desired size**
- ☐ **white glue or spray adhesive**
- ☐ **strong scissors**
- ☐ **utility knife**
- ☐ **cutting board**
- ☐ **lace, bows and ribbon**
- ☐ **tracing paper**
- ☐ **pen or pencil**

Directions:

1 Trace one of the frame patterns on page 71 onto tracing paper. Using the pattern, cut out three shapes from cardboard – one backing, one center piece and one front. Cut a piece of cardboard, approximately 2 x 4 inches for a stand.

2 Cover one side of backing piece with glue. Apply batting to this side. Trim batting to within $3/8$ inch of cardboard. Turn $3/8$-inch allowance to other side, clipping curves and excess batting at corners. Glue in place. Cover frame backing piece with fabric in same way.

3 Cover one side of center piece with fabric in same way, omitting batting.

4 Following inner line on pattern, cut out center of frame front. Cover frame front with glue, batting and fabric as for backing. Clip curves so batting and fabric will turn to wrong side without too much bulk. Trim frame front with ribbon, lace or bows as desired.

5 Glue center and backing pieces together with fabric sides out. Glue front section onto completed backing, with fabric side out. Leave top section unglued to allow picture to be inserted.

6 Cover stand with batting and fabric. Bend $1/2$ inch at one end of stand. Glue this end to back of frame at a point which allows frame to stand properly. You may wish to add a length of ribbon between stand and frame for added stability.

Trimming notes: When placing fabric, take best advantage of its print. Pre-gathered lace is easier to use for trimming than flat lace.

❖ PINCUSHION ❖

Easy: Achievable by anyone

- ☐ **small can, about $3^1/8$- 4 inches high, empty and thoroughly cleaned**
- ☐ **synthetic batting**
- ☐ **scraps of cotton print fabric**
- ☐ **about 1 foot gathered eyelet lace**

HOW TO MAKE
RIBBON ROSES

- ☐ **satin or nylon ribbon of desired width (the wider the ribbon the larger the rose will be)**
- ☐ **stem wire**
- ☐ **floral wire**
- ☐ **green floral winding tape**

1 Bend one end of stem wire to form a hook. Secure with floral wire (A).

2 Fasten end of ribbon around hook with floral wire (B).

3 Fold ribbon over hook (C) and continue winding to form bud, secure with floral wire (D).

4 To make petals, hold stem in one hand and fold ribbon toward you (E). The fold forms top of petal.

5 Turn stem counter-clockwise, winding ribbon onto bud as you turn. As ribbon straightens out after each fold make another diagonal fold as before (F). Bind end of rose with floral wire.

6 Gather end of ribbon at base of rose. Secure with floral wire (G).

7 Cover base of rose by twisting green floral tape around it.

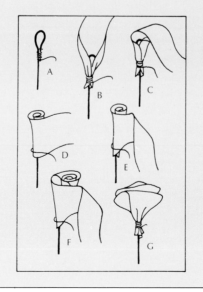

Directions:
HAIRBAND
1 Make several bows out of narrow ribbon. Glue or tie to center of hairband.
2 Tie about 2 feet of narrow ribbon around center of hairband, over center of bows, allowing ends to fall loosely. If you have a microwave oven, you can curl the ribbon, as we have done for the blue hairband (photo, page 60), by winding approximately 1 yard of slightly damp narrow ribbon around a plastic spool. Place the spool in your microwave on HIGH for approximately 30 seconds. Allow to cool then unwind. (*Note:* The lilac hairband does not have these ribbons.)
3 Glue silk leaves on either side of bows.
4 Make ribbon roses following directions on page 60, and glue to hair-band between bow loops.
5 For lilac hairband, place bows slightly off-center and glue leaves on either side of bows. Attach ribbon roses between bow loops.

BANGLES
1 Wind $3/_8$-inch-wide ribbon around bangle to cover it completely. Glue ends in place.
2 Make ribbon bows as for hairbands and tie in place.
3 Glue on leaves and ribbon roses.

COMBS
1 Make ribbon rosebuds (without petals) on wire stems. Cover stems with green floral tape. Glue to comb with green silk leaves.
2 Glue ribbon roses to center of comb over leaves and buds.

□ **satin ribbon to fit eyelets, and $1/_8$-inch-wide ribbon**
□ **white glue**
□ **pearl-headed pins**

Directions:
1 Cut out a circle of fabric large enough to cover can and a strip of batting to fit around outside of can. Glue batting in place. Place fabric circle face down with can centered on top. Draw up fabric. Fold top of fabric over edge of can and secure with glue. Fill can with batting so that it overflows at top.
2 Cut out a circle of fabric large enough to cover top of can. Place fabric over top of can. Glue it in place around side of can, folding under raw edge as you go.
3 Thread ribbon through eyelet lace. Glue lace around can, covering fabric edge.
4 Make several bows out of $1/_8$-inch-wide ribbon, gather them together with a piece of ribbon wrapped around the center and glue over ends of lace.

❖ PINE CONE PINCUSHION ❖

Easy: Achievable by anyone

□ **open pine cone**
□ **scraps coordinating cotton print fabric**
□ **cotton balls or synthetic stuffing**
□ **white glue**
□ **thread to match fabrics**
□ **$1/_8$-inch-wide ribbon**
□ **screwdriver**

Directions:
1 Cut out squares of fabric large enough to cover a cotton ball. Place one cotton ball, or equivalent size piece of stuffing, in each square, drawing up fabric corners to enclose ball. Wind thread around edges to secure. Trim away excess fabric.

2 Place a drop of glue into each opening in pine cone.
3 Using a screwdriver, push each fabric-covered ball into the pine cone.
4 Trim with ribbon bows.

❖ NO-SEW FLORAL ❖ ACCESSORIES

Easy: Achievable by anyone

□ **inexpensive plastic hairband, comb or bangle**
□ **$3/_8$-inch-wide satin or nylon ribbon and $1/_8$-inch-wide wide matching ribbon**
□ **white glue**
□ **several green silk leaves**
□ **ribbon roses (see How to Make Ribbon Roses, page 60)**
□ **green floral tape**

Pretty picture frames are always popular

❖ HAIR RIBBON HOLDER ❖

Average: For those with some experience in sewing.

- [ ] **cotton print fabric, 14 x 5$\frac{1}{8}$ inches and 24 x 1$\frac{1}{2}$ inches**
- [ ] **lightweight batting, 14 x 14$\frac{3}{8}$ inches**
- [ ] **about 28 inches ungathered lace or 14$\frac{3}{8}$ inches gathered lace**
- [ ] **about 1 foot of $\frac{1}{2}$-inch-wide elastic**
- [ ] **1$\frac{2}{3}$ yards of $\frac{1}{2}$-inch-wide satin ribbon**
- [ ] **12-inch ruler**
- [ ] **thread to match fabric**

Directions:

1 Wrap batting tightly around ruler, folding in ends and stitching to secure.
2 Gather lace (if you are using ungathered lace) and stitch to right side of one long edge of 14 x 5$\frac{1}{8}$-inch fabric.
3 Press in $\frac{3}{8}$ inch at ends of fabric. Fold fabric over batting-covered ruler, bringing long sides of fabric together. Fold in raw edge of untrimmed side and hand-stitch to lace-trimmed edge.
4 Fold 24 x 1$\frac{1}{2}$-inch strip of fabric in half with right sides facing. Stitch long side, turn and press. Insert elastic and stitch to one end of fabric. Pull up elastic, gathering fabric as you go. Secure other end.
5 Place ends of elastic piece between folded edges of fabric covering ruler. Hand-stitch in place, closing ends.
6 Cut 1$\frac{1}{4}$ yards of ribbon and fold ends into small loops. Stitch each loop to one end of ruler. Cover stitching with small bow at each end. Attach another bow at center of hanging loop.

❖ GATHERED ❖ COAT HANGER

Average: For those with some experience in sewing.

- [ ] **strip of cotton fabric, 6 inches x length of coat hanger plus 10 inches**
- [ ] **6-inch-long bias strip of fabric or ribbon**
- [ ] **ribbon**
- [ ] **synthetic batting**
- [ ] **wooden coat hanger**
- [ ] **thread to match fabric**

Directions:

1 If possible, remove hook from hanger. It will be reinserted later. Cut strips of batting about 2 inches wide and wind them around wood part of hanger. Stitch ends to secure.
2 Fold large fabric strip in half lengthwise, with right sides facing and raw edges even. Stitch long and one short side. Turn.
3 Stitch gathering rows along both long sides. Slide cover onto hanger. Pull up

gathering threads to fit. Hand-stitch open end closed.
4 Fold bias strip in half lengthwise with right sides together. Stitch long and one short side. Turn to right side. Slide over hook. Hand-stitch to secure. Or, wind ribbon around hook to conceal it and stitch to secure. Insert hook into hanger through all thicknesses of fabric.
5 Trim hanger with a ribbon bow.

❖ COAT HANGER WITH ❖ GATHERED TOP

Average: For those with some experience in sewing.

- [ ] **$\frac{1}{4}$ yard of 43-inch-wide fabric**
- [ ] **synthetic batting**
- [ ] **6-inch-long bias strip of fabric or ribbon**
- [ ] **ribbon**
- [ ] **wooden coat hanger**
- [ ] **thread to match fabric**

Directions:

1 Cut two pieces of fabric, each 15$\frac{1}{8}$ x 3$\frac{1}{2}$ inches for upper part of hanger and two pieces, each 9$\frac{1}{8}$ x 3$\frac{1}{2}$ inches for lower part. Round off one end of each piece uniformly. Cover is made in two halves, then joined in the middle.
2 If possible, remove hook from hanger. It will be reinserted later. Cut batting into 2-inch-wide strips and wind them around wood. Hand-stitch ends to secure.
3 Stitch a gathering row along long sides and around curved ends of upper pieces. Draw up gathering to fit length of lower pieces.
4 Stitch upper and lower fabric pieces together, with right sides facing and raw edges even, leaving straight ends open. Turn. Slide both pieces onto hanger, turning in raw edges at center. Hand-stitch pieces together at center.
5 Fold bias strip in half lengthwise with right sides facing. Stitch long and one short side. Turn. Slide over hook. Or, wind ribbon around hook to conceal it and stitch to secure. Insert hook into hanger.
6 Tie ribbon around hanger to conceal stitching. Tie bow around hook.

❖ FLAT COAT HANGER ❖ COVER

Average: For those with some experience in sewing.

- [ ] **strip of cotton fabric, approximately 16 x 20 inches**

- [ ] **lace and ribbon trims**
- [ ] **6-inch-long bias strip or ribbon**
- [ ] **synthetic batting**
- [ ] **wooden coat hanger**
- [ ] **thread to match fabric**

Directions:

1 Cut batting into 2-inch-wide strips and wind them around wood. Hand-stitch to secure.

2 Fold fabric in half lengthwise and place wrapped wood on top of double layer of fabric. Starting $\frac{1}{2}$-inch from top of hanger and using photo as a guide, draw hanger cover shape around top curve and ends of hanger. Continue drawing rest of cover shape extending $4\frac{3}{8}$ inches beyond bottom of hanger. Cut out.

3 Place cover sections together, with right sides facing and raw edges even. Stitch around curved edge, leaving small break in stitching for inserting hook.

4 At lower edge turn in $\frac{1}{4}$ inch and then another $\frac{1}{4}$ inch. Stitch a hem. Trim with lace.

5 Fold bias strip in half lengthwise, with right sides facing and raw edges even. Stitch long and one short side. Turn. Slide over hook. Or, wind ribbon around hook to conceal it. Slip cover over hanger. Insert hook and hand-stitch bias or ribbon to secure. Trim hanger with a ribbon bow.

❖ SCENTED SHOE STUFFERS ❖

Easy: Achievable by anyone.

- ☐ $\frac{1}{4}$ yard of 43-inch-wide cotton fabric
- ☐ synthetic stuffing, lavender or potpourri
- ☐ lace and ribbon
- ☐ thread to match fabric
- ☐ tracing paper and pencil

Directions:

1 Trace pattern on page 93 and use it to cut four shapes from fabric. With right sides facing and raw edges even, stitch 2 fabric shapes together around curved edge. Clip seams. Turn and press. Repeat for other two shapes

2 At raw edge turn under $\frac{1}{8}$ inch and then another $\frac{1}{4}$ inch. Stitch a hem. Trim with lace if desired.

3 Fill shoe stuffers with synthetic stuffing, lavender or potpourri. Tie bows made from ribbon or self-fabric bias around tops to secure.

❖ TEDDY BEAR ❖

Average: For those with some experience in sewing.

- ☐ $\frac{1}{4}$ yard of 43-inch-wide cotton fabric
- ☐ synthetic stuffing
- ☐ two small beads or buttons
- ☐ embroidery floss to match fabric
- ☐ $\frac{1}{8}$-inch-wide ribbon
- ☐ sewing thread to match fabric
- ☐ tracing paper and pencil
- ☐ doll's straw hat (optional)

Clockwise from top left: Hangers with gathered tops (2), flat hanger cover, gathered hanger, hair ribbon holder, shoe stuffers

Directions:

1 Trace and cut out pattern pieces following red outlines. All pieces are joined with right sides facing. Clip all curved seams for ease.

2 Stitch pairs of arm and leg pieces together, leaving upper straight edges open. Turn and stuff firmly.

3 Stitch pairs of body pieces together along one curved edge. Stitch these constructions together to form body, leaving upper straight edge open. Turn and stuff firmly.

4 Stitch pairs of ear pieces together around curved edges. Turn. Turn in $1/4$ inch on open raw edge. Press. Stuff lightly.

5 Stitch head center back and center front seams. Join head front and back constructions. Clip seam, turn and stuff firmly.

6 Using doubled thread, stitch a gathering row around open edge of each body piece. Pull up gathering to close. Secure. Stitch arms, legs and head to body. Legs may be attached in sitting or standing position (see photo). Stitch ears to head.

7 Embroider satin-stitch nose and straight-stitch mouth, using photo as a guide. Stitch on beads or buttons for eyes.

8 To complete your bear, add a ribbon bow around its neck. A doll's straw hat is a sweet touch.

❖ MOUSE ❖

Average: For those with some experience in sewing.

- ☐ **6 inches of 43-inch-wide cotton fabric**
- ☐ **small piece of fusible interfacing**
- ☐ **synthetic stuffing**
- ☐ **two small beads**
- ☐ **buttontwist thread or dental floss for whiskers**
- ☐ **$1/8$-inch-wide satin ribbon**
- ☐ **sewing thread to match fabric**
- ☐ **tracing paper and pencil**

Directions:

1 Trace and cut out pattern pieces following black outlines.

2 Iron interfacing to ear pieces. Place

Make teddies and mice in cheery prints

ear pieces together, in pairs, with right sides facing. Stitch around curved edges. Clip seams, turn and press. Turn in $1/4$ inch at open raw edge. Press.

3 Place long raw edges of tail together with right sides of fabric facing. Stitch, leaving straight edge open for turning. Turn and stuff firmly.

4 Stitch darts in body pieces. Place body pieces together with right sides facing. Stitch around body, leaving opening for stuffing and attaching tail. Stitch body to base matching markings and leaving an opening for stuffing. Stuff body. Tuck tail into opening and hand-stitch into place, closing opening as you go.

5 Make a $3/8$-inch pleat in each ear. Attach ears to head.

6 Stitch on bead eyes.

7 Stitch through snout with several strands of buttontwist thread or dental floss. Clip to form whiskers.

8 Tie a ribbon bow around neck.

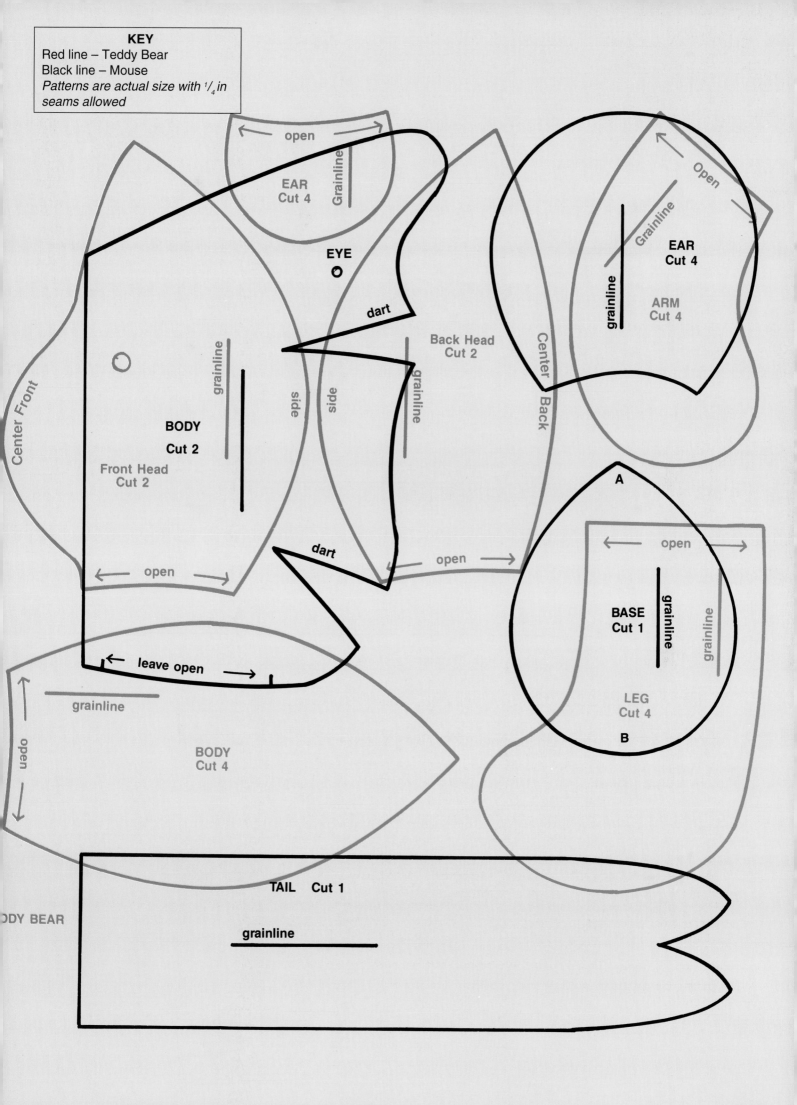

KEY
Red line – Teddy Bear
Black line – Mouse
Patterns are actual size with ¹/₄ in seams allowed

open

EAR
Cut 4

Grainline

EYE

Open

Grainline

EAR
Cut 4

grainline

ARM
Cut 4

dart

Back Head
Cut 2

Center Back

grainline

side

side

grainline

BODY
Cut 2

Front Head
Cut 2

Center Front

A

open

dart

open

grainline

BASE
Cut 1

grainline

LEG
Cut 4

leave open

B

grainline

open

BODY
Cut 4

TAIL   Cut 1

grainline

DY BEAR

MOUSE

interfacing. Iron interfacing to wrong side of all pattern pieces.

2 Place main and contrasting fabric wings together with wrong sides facing. Stitch all around, $\frac{1}{4}$ inch from edge. Trim fabric close to stitching. Stitch again all around edge with zigzag stitch, covering previous stitching. Hand-stitch feather lines on wings with straight stitching.

3 Cut out wing openings in sides of chicken. Stitch around wing openings. Trim fabric close to stitching. Zigzag stitch over previous stitching as for wings. Stitch wings onto chicken above openings, along marked lines, with contrasting fabric on wing undersides.

4 Place beak pieces and comb pieces together with wrong sides facing. Stitch around edges. Trim fabric close to stitching. Zigzag stitch around edges, covering previous stitching. Pin beak and comb into position on right side of one chicken body piece, keeping raw edges even.

5 Place two chicken body pieces together with right sides facing. Stitch around curved edges, leaving lower edge open. Clip seams. Turn and press.

6 Turn in $\frac{1}{4}$ inch along raw lower edge. Turn in another $\frac{1}{2}$ inch. Stitch to form casing, leaving opening for elastic. Thread elastic through casing. Place cover on basket to adjust elastic. Secure ends of elastic. Close opening by hand.

Make our egg basket cover, oven mitt and potholder as a set in coordinating fabrics

❖ SEWING KIT ❖

Average: For those with some experience in sewing.

- [ ] **two pieces of double-sided quilted fabric, one 6 x 8³/₄ inches the other 6 x 4 inches**
- [ ] **1¹/₄ yards of bias binding**
- [ ] **sewing supplies to equip kit**
- [ ] **thread to match fabric**

Directions:

1 Bind one 6-inch edge of smaller rectangle with bias binding. Place this piece on larger piece, with wrong sides together and raw edges matching. Pin in place. Round off all corners. Stitch around edge, securing pocket corners.

2 Fold two 7¹/₈-inch lengths of bias binding in half lengthwise. Stitch. Knot one end of each strip. Stitch other ends to inside center top and bottom of kit as shown in photo.

3 Bind all around edge of sewing kit with remaining bias binding, enclosing ends of ties as you go.

4 Stitch down center of pocket, through all thicknesses, dividing it in two.

❖ EGG BASKET COVER ❖

Average: For those with some experience in sewing.

- [ ] **¹/₂ yard of 43-inch- wide cotton fabric**
- [ ] **scrap of contrasting cotton fabric**
- [ ] **16 x 32-inch piece of fusible interfacing**
- [ ] **³/₈-inch wide elastic**
- [ ] **open basket about 7¹/₈ inches in diameter**
- [ ] **thread to match fabric**
- [ ] **tracing paper and pencil**

Directions:

1 Trace and cut out the chicken, wing, beak and comb patterns on page 93. Cut out two chickens each from main fabric and interfacing. Cut out two wings each from main fabric, contrasting fabric and interfacing. Cut two beaks and two combs each from contrasting fabric and

❖ OVEN MITT ❖

Average: For those with some experience in sewing.

☐ **quilted cotton, 12 x 16 inches**
☐ **contrasting fabric 8 inches square**
☐ **strip of another contrasting fabric 2 x 14³/₄ inches**
☐ **4 inches of bias binding or fabric**
☐ **thread to match fabric**

Directions:

1   Trace and cut out two mitts and two constrasting bands following the patterns on page 93. With raw edges matching and with right sides of bands facing wrong sides of mitts, stitch bands to mitts. Press bands to right side. Trim raw edge with second contrasting fabric strip or braid. Trim and tack down any raw edges.

2   Make a loop of bias binding and attach to corner of right side of one mitt piece with raw edges even.

3   Place two mitt shapes together with right sides facing. Stitch around curved edge, reinforcing stitching at fork of thumb and finger. Clip seam for ease. Turn and press.

❖ TWO-HANDED ❖ POTHOLDER

Average: For those with some experience in sewing.

☐ **piece of quilted fabric 16 x 29¹/₈ inches**

Above: Make our shower cap, toiletry bag and toilet paper holder in complementary country calicos.

☐ **two pieces of contrasting fabric, each 8³/₄ x 8 inches**
☐ **16-inch strip of contrasting fabric or braid**
☐ **thread to match fabric**

Directions:

1   Cut quilted fabric in half lengthwise, so that each piece is 8 x 29¹/₈ inches.

2   Trim one 8-inch end of each contrasting fabric strip with second contrasting fabric or braid, enclosing raw edge.

3   Place quilted fabric pieces and contrasting fabric pieces together. Round off all corners. Place contrasting fabric pieces on each end of one quilted section so that wrong side of contrasting piece faces right side of quilted piece. Place other quilted piece on top so that right sides of quilted pieces are facing. Stitch all around, leaving a small opening for turning near center. Clip seam. Turn and press. Close opening by hand.

Left: Simple-to-sew sewing kit

❖ SHOWER CAP ❖

Average: For those with some experience in sewing.

☐ **²/₃ yard each of 43-inch-wide cotton fabric and plastic sheeting**
☐ **two 2¹/₄-yard-long pieces of bias binding (one may be cotton fabric)**
☐ **³/₈-inch-wide elastic**
☐ **thread to match fabric**
☐ **compass**

Directions:

1   Using the compass, draw a circle, 24 inches in diameter, on fabric and plastic. Cut out circles.

2   Place plastic on wrong side of fabric. Stitch around outside edge. Trim close to stitching.

3   Bind edge with bias binding. Stitch second length of bias binding around inside, 2¹/₄ inches from edge, to form casing for elastic.

7 Wind ribbon around curtain ring to cover it. Glue ends to secure. Fold loop around ring, concealing ends of ribbon beneath loop. Glue to secure. Hand-stitch ends of loop to wrong side of holder, at point. Trim with small ribbon bow.
8 Stitch across holder halfway between hand-stitching and lower folded edge, dividing it into two compartments. Slip a roll of toilet paper in each compartment.

❖ APPLIQUED TOWELS ❖

Easy: Achievable by anyone.

- [ ] **towel**
- [ ] **scrap of cotton print fabric**
- [ ] **fusible interfacing**
- [ ] **thread to contrast with fabric**
- [ ] **tracing paper and pencil**

Directions:
1 Following the designs on page 58, trace and cut out appliqué patterns. From bonding fabric cut exact shape of motif to be appliquéd. Baste to wrong side of cotton fabric. Cut around motif, leaving $1/4$-inch seam allowance.
2 Baste appliqué to towel. Iron in place.
3 Stitch around motif, $1/4$-inch from edge, with tight zigzag stitch. Trim away any excess fabric. Stitch around appliqué with a slightly wider zigzag stitch, covering previous stitching and raw edges.

❖ PLACE MATS WITH ❖ CONTRASTING CENTERS

Average: For those with some experience in sewing.

These two place mats are made following the same basic instructions, but one has a single-piece contrasting center while the other has a contrasting center panel made from strips of coordinating fabrics.

- [ ] **cotton fabric 20 x 25$1/8$ inches**
- [ ] **synthetic batting, 14$3/8$ x 25$1/8$ inches**
- [ ] **contrasting fabric 16 x 10$3/8$ inches**

APPLIQUE TIPS

Choose pure cotton, silk or linen fabrics for the motif. Synthetics may be slippery and difficult to handle. If you use all cotton fabrics, use a pure cotton sewing thread to avoid damage from high-temperature ironing.

Above left: Beautifully appliquéd towels

❖ TOILETRY BAG ❖

Average: For those with some experience in sewing.

- [ ] **pieces of cotton fabric and plastic sheeting, each 24 x 11$1/8$ inches**
- [ ] **1$3/4$ yards of $1/2$-inch-wide satin ribbon**
- [ ] **thread to match fabric**

Directions:
1 Fold fabric in half lengthwise, with right sides together. Stitch sides. Repeat for plastic.
2 Turn fabric bag right side out. Trim 2 inches from top of plastic bag. Slip plastic bag inside fabric bag.
3 Turn in $1/4$ inch at top edge of fabric bag. Turn in another 2 inches to cover edge of plastic bag. Stitch through all thicknesses along fold and again $1/2$ inch away to form casing.
4 Open stitching on outside of fabric side seams between casing lines on outside. Cut length of ribbon in half. Thread half through one opening, through casing and out the other opening. Repeat with other ribbon around other side.
5 Knot ends of ribbon together.

❖ TOILET PAPER HOLDER ❖

Average: For those with some experience in sewing.

- [ ] **two strips of cotton fabric, each 1 yard x 11$1/8$ inches**
- [ ] **strip of fusible interfacing 1 yard x 11$1/8$ inches**
- [ ] **3$1/2$ yards of $1/2$-inch-wide lace**
- [ ] **1$2/3$ yards of $1/8$-inch-wide satin ribbon**
- [ ] **small wooden curtain ring**
- [ ] **white glue**
- [ ] **thread to match fabric**
- [ ] **2 rolls of toilet paper**

Directions:
1 Iron on interfacing to one fabric strip. Trim one end of each fabric strip to a point.
2 Stitch two 24-inch-long rows of lace down center of the interfaced fabric strip, beginning at pointed end and with straight edges of lace meeting in center. Stitch ribbon over straight edges of lace, covering the edges.
3 With raw edges even, stitch lace, on right side, around all sides of lace-trimmed piece, pleating lace at point and corners for ease.
4 Place fabric pieces together, with right sides facing and raw edges even. Stitch, following stitching line made for lace, leaving straight end open for turning. Trim fabric at points and corners. Turn and press.
5 Turn under $3/8$ inch on straight end. Hand-stitch this end to wrong side, below point and even with corners.
6 Cut strip of leftover fabric 4$3/4$ x 1$1/8$ inches for loop. Fold strip in half lengthwise. Stitch long side. Turn and press. Topstitch length of strip with four rows of stitching.

- ☐ 1²/₃ yards contrasting bias binding
- ☐ thread to match or contrast with fabrics

Directions:

1 For the dark print place mat, we quilted the center panel by outline-stitching the fabric pattern with gold thread. To do this, baste batting on wrong side of center panel. Stitch through all thicknesses. Place batting and center panel centered on wrong side of place mat.

For ecru striped place mat, make a center panel by stitching contrasting fabric together. Press. Place batting on wrong side of place mat. Place center panel in place over batting and baste through all thicknesses.

2 Fold and cut corners as shown in diagram A (page 69). Stitch to miter corners, stitching up to ³/₈ inch from edge. Press seams open.

3 Fold corners to right side. Turn under ³/₈ inch along raw edges. Place bias binding under folded edges. Stitch down through all thicknesses. Press.

❖ PLACE MAT WITH ❖ SHAPED CORNERS

Average: For those with some experience in sewing.

- ☐ two pieces of cotton fabric 18³/₄ x 13¹/₈ inches
- ☐ synthetic batting 18³/₄ x 13¹/₈ inches
- ☐ fabric scraps in three colors for appliqué

Directions:

1 Trim away triangles evenly from corners of batting and fabric. Baste batting to wrong side of one fabric piece.

2 Trace the palm tree pattern on page 70 and use it to cut out appliqué motif from fabric scraps. Appliqué design to fabric piece with batting, following instructions given for towels (page 68).

3 Position place mat pieces together with right sides facing. Stitch around outside edge, leaving opening for turning. Clip corners. Turn and press.

4 Stitch with a double row of stitches around shape of place mat and again ³/₄ inch away.

❖ TABLE NAPKIN WITH ❖ CONTRASTING BORDER

Average: For those with some experience in sewing.

- ☐ firm cotton fabric 18³/₄ inches square

- ☐ contrasting fabric, four border strips each 18³/₄ x 2³/₄ inches
- ☐ second contrasting fabric, four strips 1¹/₈ x 18³/₄ inches folded in half lengthwise; or piping or bias binding

Directions:

1 Fold in ³/₈ inch along one edge of each border strip. Cut ends to perfect diagonals and join to form a square as shown in B.

2 Place right side of border against wrong side of square, edges matching. Stitch around edge. Trim corners, turn and press.

3 Place fabric strips or piping under inner border. Stitch through all thicknesses.

❖ TABLE NAPKIN WITH ❖ EMBROIDERED TRIM

Easy: Achievable by anyone.

- ☐ 22¹/₈-inch square of firm cotton fabric
- ☐ thread to contrast with fabric

Directions:

1 Cut away corners of fabric as shown in diagram C.

2 Fold and stitch up to ³/₈ inch from end as shown. Turn and press. Turn under ³/₈ inch around raw edges. Press. Stitch using a decorative machine stitch. See diagram D.

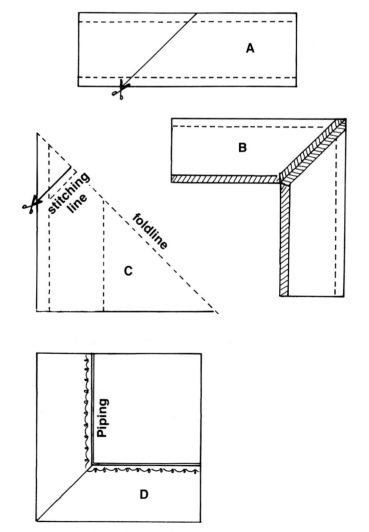

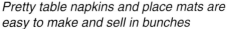

Pretty table napkins and place mats are easy to make and sell in bunches

APPLIQUE BOWS

PLACE MAT APPLIQUE

70

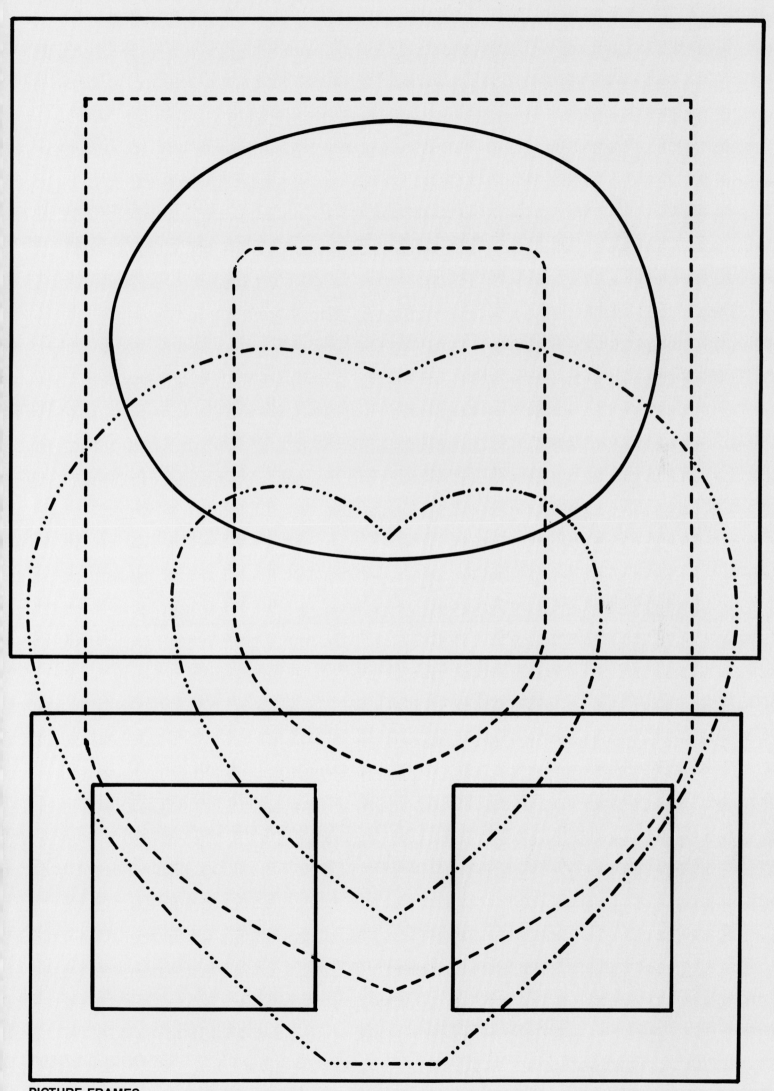

PICTURE FRAMES

Gift treasures

Perfect gifts for all occasions, beautifully presented and gift wrapped, are always in demand at fairs. Next to the delicate knitted and beautifully embroidered items be sure to include a raffle prize, such as our lovely Victorian Rose pillow, and some special treasures for Christmas.

All the hints for planning your craft booth also apply to the gift booth. Organize your team meeting as soon as you can. It will give you a chance to get to know your team and their special skills. Willing helpers may need assistance to find projects that suit their levels of skill. Make sure there is a wide variety of items to make, ranging from the very simple to the challenging. Never turn away a willing worker! Cooperative projects are very good for those with little time or a little less skill. Introduce a capable sewer to someone who can't sew but who can cut out patterns and you have a productive little unit.

You will also need to make decisions about materials – should they be bought or donated? Generally, it is not a good idea to make gift items out of old bits of leftovers, unless they are particularly pretty. Buying materials will allow you to have some control over the overall look of the booth and to coordinate items with one another.

Draw up a master plan, showing all the items to be made. Give one to each team member with his or her own contribution highlighted.

Make copies of patterns, and include clear instructions for everyone. The instructions should list the materials required, including trims and special wrappings for each project.

There should be a clear timetable available to all team members, showing expected completion dates for various projects, collection and packaging days. Organize the schedule so there is sufficient time to inspect items. Gifts must be well made and neatly finished. Wrapping gift items is particularly important. Choose appropriate "see-through" wrappings and decorate as extravagantly as you like with colored ribbons.

Sewing or packaging days, when the team can get together to exchange ideas and share the work, are a great idea and always good fun. Plan ahead and have a fairly clear idea of what you want to accomplish on the day.

PRICES

Beautiful handmade gifts are very popular and can fetch quite a good price. Often they are items which are impossible to buy except at a fair or bazaar, such as embroidered, hand-knitted bed socks for a favorite Aunt or a truly decorative draft stopper for the home.

DECORATION

The decor of your gift booth should reflect all the fun of the fair – aim for lots of color with drapes of fabric, clouds of balloons and a bright banner identifying your booth. Cover the counter with fabric or pretty paper before displaying the gift items, attractively arranged or gathered into pretty baskets. Don't crowd your booth; keep extras nearby to fill in as needed. Stock a supply of plastic or paper bags to hold purchases.

A B B R E V I A T I O N S
KNITTING AND CROCHET

K = Knit
P = Purl
st st = stockinette stitch
rep = repeat
rem = remain
inc = increase
dec = decrease
pat = pattern
foll = following
alt = alternate
tog = together
rs = right side
ws = wrong side
yo = yarn over
psso = pass slipped stitch over
sl st = slip stitch
ch = chain
dc = double crochet
tr = triple crochet

A selection of gift treasures

❖
BED SOCKS

Average: For those with some experience in knitting.

To fit average foot

MATERIALS

Synthetic worsted-weight yarn (50 g) 3 balls; 1 pair Size 6 knitting needles and a spare Size 8) knitting needle; 1/8-inch-wide ribbon; scraps of lightweight yarn (optional); tapestry needle.

GAUGE

On Size 6 needles in stockinette stitch (st st) – 11st = 2"; 8 rows = 1".

Directions:

Using Size 6 needles, cast on 46 sts.
Row 1: K2, *P2, K2, rep from * to end.
Row 2: P2, *K2, P2, rep from * to end.
Rep Rows 1 and 2 until rib measures 6½" from beg, ending with Row 2 and inc one st each end of last row – 48 sts.
Proceed as follows:
Note: When turning, bring yarn to front of work, slip next st onto right hand needle, yarn back, slip st back onto left hand needle, then turn and proceed as instructed. This avoids holes in work.
Row 1: K32, turn. Row 2: K16, turn.
Work 50 rows in garter st (K every row) on these 16 sts. Break off yarn.
With right side facing, join yarn to rem sts on right hand needle and pick up and K 27 sts from side of instep, then pick up and K 8 sts across top of instep (toe sts).
Using a double pointed needle, knit rem 8 sts across top of instep (toe sts), pick up and K 27 sts from other side of instep, then knit across rem sts – 102 sts.
Work 17 rows in garter st.
Next row: K1, 2tog, 46, (2tog) twice, 46, 2tog, 1 – 98 sts. Cont in this manner, dec at each end of both needles in every row until 86 sts rem. Bind off.

FINISHING

Using a flat seam, sew foot and leg seams, reversing seam for half of ribbing if desired. Fold ribbing to right side.
If you like, use the lightweight yarn scraps and tapestry needle to embroider roses on the insteps. Follow the grub rose diagram on page 70 and use straight stitches. Trim with a ribbon bow.

❖
TEA COZY

Average: For those with some experience in knitting.

Fits medium teapot

MATERIALS

Synthetic worsted-weight yarn (50 g): 2 balls; 1 pair of Size 6 knitting needles; cable needle; tapestry needle.

GAUGE

On Size 6 needles in stockinette stitch (st st) – 11 sts = 2"; 8 rows = 11".

SPECIAL ABBREVIATIONS

C2F – Slip next 2 sts onto a cable needle and hold in front of work, 2, then 2 from cable needle.
C2B – Slip next 2 sts onto a cable needle and hold in back of work, 2, then 2 from cable needle.
C4F – Slip next st onto cable needle and hold in front of work, 3, then 1 from cable needle.
C4B – Slip next 3 sts onto a cable needle and hold in back of work, 1, then 3 from cable needle.

Directions:

First Half
Using Size 6 needles, cast on 56 sts.
Knit 5 rows.
Begin pattern as follows:
Row 1: P3, K4, P3, K9, P3, K4, P4, K4, P3, K9, P3, K4, P3.
Row 2: K3, P4, K3, P9, K3, P4, K4, P4, K3, P9, K3, P4, K3.
Row 3: P3, C2F, P3, C4F, K1, C4B, P3, C2B, P4, C2F, P3, C4F, K1, C4B, P3, C2B, P3.
Row 4: K3, P4, K3, P9, K3, P4, K4, P4, K3, P9, K3, P4, K3.
Rows 1 thru 4 form pattern stitch.
Work 24 rows in pattern stitch.
Top Shaping:
Keeping in pattern as established, work as follows: Next row: P2tog, work next 23 st in pat st, K2tog, work in pat st to last 2 sts, 2tog.
Work even in pat st for 1 row.
Cont to dec in center and at each end of next and every other row until 29 sts rem.
Work even in pat st for 1 row.
Next row: K1, *2tog, rep from * to end.
Draw yarn through rem sts and fasten off securely.
Second Half: Work same as First Half.

FINISHING

Using a flat seam, sew side seams of cozy halves together, leaving openings for spout and handle. Make twisted cords. With cord, form loops and stitch to top.

❖
COAT HANGER COVER

Average: For those with some experience in knitting.

To fit standard wooden coat hanger

MATERIALS

Synthetic sport-weight yarn (50 g): 1 ball for each hanger; 1 pair Size 5 knitting needles; wooden coat hanger; synthetic batting; white glue and plastic tubing (optional); ribbon and silk flowers (or trims as desired); tapestry needle.

GAUGE

On Size 5 needles in stockinette stitch (st st) – 13sts = 2"; 9 rows = 1".

Directions:

Using Size 5 needles, cast on 18 sts.
Work 4 rows st st (K 1 row, P 1 row).
Work 6 rows garter st (K every row).
**Row 11: K1, inc once in each of next 16 sts, K1 – 34 sts.
Work 7 rows st st, beg with a purl row.
Row 19: K1, (2tog) 16 times, K1 – 18 sts.
Work 5 rows garter st.**
Rep from ** to ** until work measures approx 8" from beg, ending with Row 19 of pattern.
Work 3 rows garter st.
Tie a colored thread at each end of last row to mark center.
Work 2 rows garter st.
Rep from ** to ** until work measures approx 15" from beg, ending with 5 rows of garter st. Be sure you have the same number of pattern rows as on the other side of the center.
Work 4 rows st st. Bind off loosely.

FINISHING

Stitch up long side and one short end of cover. Remove hook from hanger and cover wooden section with batting, using stitching or glue to secure batting. Insert hanger into cover and stitch other short end closed. Cover hook with plastic tubing, or wind length of yarn around hook, then secure hook in top hole. Decorate with ribbon and silk flowers, using photo as a guide.

For avid knitters, bed socks, coat hangers and tea cozy are quick to make

❖ BABY'S CARDIGAN AND CAP

Challenging: Requires more experience in knitting.

Size:	**Newborn**	**6 mos**	**9 mos**
Body Chest:	14½"	16"	18"
Finished Measurements:			
Chest:	16"	18"	20"

Directions are given for **Newborn** size. Changes for sizes **6 mos** and **9 mos** are in parentheses.

A new baby layette features cardigan, cap, pullover and booties

MATERIALS

Fingering-weight 3-ply yarn (50 g): 2 (3, 3) balls for cardigan and 1 ball for cap; 1 pair each Size 3 and Size 2 knitting needles; 5 stitch holders; 4 buttons for cardigan; 28" of 3/8"-wide satin ribbon for cap; tapestry needle; sewing thread to match yarn; sewing needle.

GAUGE

On Size 3 needles in stockinette st (st st) – 8 sts = 1"; 11 rows = 1", and 2 pattern repeats = 2¼".

Directions:
JACKET (Worked in one piece to underarm)
Using Size 3 needles, cast on 191 (207, 223) sts.

Work 8 rows in garter st (K every row)
Note: First row is wrong side.
Next row: K6, slip these 6 sts onto a length of yarn, knit to last 6 sts, turn, slip rem 6 sts on another length of yarn – 179 (195, 211) sts.
Beg pattern:
Row 1 (right side): K1, 2tog, *yo, K5, yo, sl 1, K2tog; psso, rep from * to last 8 sts, yo, K5, yo, sl 1, K1, psso, K1.
Row 2 and all even-numbered rows: Purl.
Row 3: Rep Row 1.
Row 5: K3, *yo, sl 1, K1, psso, K1, 2tog, yo, K3, rep from * to end.
Row 7: K1, K2tog, yo, K1, *yo, sl 1, K2tog, psso, yo, K1, rep from * to last 3 sts, yo, sl 1, 1, psso, 1.
Row 8: Rep Row 2.
Rows 1 to 8 form pattern stitch.

Cont in pat, until work measures approx 4½ (6½, 7½)" from beg, ending with Row 8.

Divide for right front

Row 1: Work first 45 (49, 53) st in pat. Turn.

Continue in pat and work 22 (24, 26) rows more.

Next row: P4 (2, 5), (2tog) 18 (22, 22) times, 5 (3, 4) – 27 (27, 31) sts.

Break off yarn, leave sts on a stitch holder. With right side facing, join yarn to next 89 (97, 105) sts for Back.

Work 23 (25, 27) rows in pat.

Next row: P7, (2tog) 37 (41, 45) times, P8 – 52 (56, 60) sts.

Break off yarn, leave sts on a stitch holder. With right side facing, join yarn to rem sts and work Left Front to correspond with

Right Front.

Sleeves

On Size 2 needles, cast on 32 (37, 37) sts. Work 6 rows in garter st (Row 1 is wrong side).

Next row: K6(7, 7), inc one st in each of next 19 (22, 22) sts, K7 (8, 8) – 51 (59, 59) sts.

Change to Size 3 needles.

Work in patt as for Jacket until work measures approx 5 (5½, 6½)" from beg, ending with Row 8.

Tie a colored thread at each end of last row to mark it.

Work 23 (25, 27) rows in pat.

Next row: P3 (1, 1), (P2tog, P1) 15 (19, 19) times, P3 (1, 1) – 36 (40, 40) sts.

Break off yarn, leave sts on a stitch holder.

Yoke

With wrong side facing, slip sts from stitch holders onto a Size 3 needle in this order: Left Front, 1st Sleeve, Back, 2nd Sleeve, then Right Front – 178 (190, 202) sts.

Row 1: K1, K2tog, *K2, K2tog, rep from * to last 3 sts, K1, K2tog – 133 (142, 151) sts.

Row 2: Knit 1 row.

Row 3: K5 (4, 3), (K2tog, K9) 11 (12, 13) times, K2tog, knit to end – 121 (129, 137) sts.

Rows 4 to 6: Knit 3 rows.

Row 7: K5 (4, 3), (K2tog, K8) 11 (12, 13) times, K2tog, knit to end – 109 (116, 123) sts.

Rows 8 to 10: Knit 3 rows.

Row 11: K4 (3, 2), (K2tog, K7) 11 (12, 13) times, K2tog, knit to end –97 (103, 109) sts.

Rows 12 to 14: Knit 3 rows.

Row 15: K4 (3, 2), (K2tog, K6) 11 (12, 13) times, K2tog, knit to end – 85 (90, 95) sts.

Rows 16 to 18: Knit 3 rows.

Row 19: K3 (2, 1), (K2tog, K5) 11 (12, 13) times, K2tog, knit to end – 73 (77, 81) sts.

Rows 20 to 22: Knit 3 rows.

Row 23: K3 (2, 1), (K2tog, K4) 11 (12, 13) times, K2tog, K2 (1, 0) – 61 (64, 67) sts.

Knit 1 row. Break off yarn.

Leave sts on stitch holder.

Left Front Band

Slip 6 sts from length of yarn onto a Size 2 needle. Join yarn to inside edge, inc in first st, knit to end.

Cont in garter st, until band is long enough to fit (slightly stretched) along front edge to top of yoke, ending with a wrong side.

Right Front Band

Work as for Left Front Band to within 24 rows.

**Next row: K3, bind off 2 sts, K2.

Next row: K2, cast on 2 sts, K3.

Knit 8 rows.**

Rep from ** to ** once, then rep buttonhole rows once – 3 buttonholes made.

Knit 3 rows.

Leave sts on needle. Do not break off yarn.

Neckband

On the Size 2 needle that has Right Front Band sts on it, knit across sts from stitch holder, then knit across sts from Left Front Band – 75 (78, 81) sts.

Knit 4 rows garter st, working a buttonhole (as before) in Rows 2 and 3. Bind off.

FINISHING

Using backstitch, join sleeve seams to colored threads, then join rem seam to body. Stitch front bands in position. Stitch on buttons.

CAP

On the Size 3 needles, cast on 75 (83, 91) sts.

Work 5 rows in garter st (Row 1 is wrong side).

Work 39 (47, 55) rows pat as for Cardigan.

Newborn and 9 mos Sizes Only – dec (inc) one st at each end of last row –73 (83, 93) sts.

Crown shaping:

Row 1: K9 (11, 17), (K2tog, K10) 5 (6, 5) times, (K2tog) 2 (0, 0) times, K0 (0, 16) – 66 (77, 88) sts.

Row 2 and all even-numbered rows: Knit.

Row 3: (K2tog, K9) 6 (7, 8) times – 60 (70, 80) sts.

Row 5: (K2tog, K8) 6 (7, 8) times – 54 (63, 72) sts.

Row 7: (K2tog, K7) 5 (7, 8) times – 48 (56, 64) sts.

Cont to dec in this manner in alt rows until 12 (14, 16) sts rem.

Break off yarn. Pull end through rem sts, draw up and fasten off securely.

FINISHING

Using a flat seam, sew seam beg 1" from crown. With sewing thread, attach ribbon to each side of cap.

❖
BOOTIES

Average: For those with some experience in knitting.

To fit sizes 0-6 months
Note: For slightly smaller booties, use needles one size smaller than those which give correct gauge. For slightly larger booties, use needles one size larger than those which give correct gauge.

MATERIALS
Fingering-weight 3 Ply yarn (50g): 1 ball of white for Garter Stitch Booties and 1 ball each of white (MC) and pink (C), or desired contrasting color, for Booties with Ribbed Ankle; 1 pair Size 3 needles; about 1 yard of $1/4$" wide ribbon for each pair; tapestry needle.

GAUGE
On Size 3 needles in stockinette stitch (st st) – 8 sts = 1"; 11 rows= 1".

Directions:
GARTER STITCH BOOTIES
On Size 3 needles with white, cast on 43 sts.
Row 1: (K1, inc in next st, K18, inc in next st) twice, K1.
Row 2 and all even rows: Knit.
Row 3: (K1, inc in next st, K20, inc in next st) twice, K1.
Row 5: (K1, inc in next st, K22, inc in next st) twice, K1.
Row 7: (K1, inc in next st, K24, inc in next st) twice, K1.
Row 9: (K1, inc in next st, K26, inc in next st) twice, K1.
Row 11: (K1, inc in next st, K28, inc in next st) twice, K1 – 67 sts.
Row 12: K2tog, K63, K2tog. 65sts. ***
Work 10 rows in st st (K1 row , P 1 row).
Shaping:
Next row: K37, K2tog, turn.
Next row: Sl 1, K9, K2tog, turn.
Rep last row until 45 sts rem (17 sts on each side of instep).
Next row: K10, K2tog, then knit to end.
Next row: Purl – 44 sts.
Ankle:
Next row: K1, *yo, K2tog; rep from * to last st, K1.
Next row: Purl, inc one st in center st – 45 sts.
Next row: K2, *P1, K1, rep from * to last st, K1.
Next row: K1, *P1, K1, rep from * to end.
Rep last 2 rows 3 times.
Work 14 rows in garter st (K every row). Bind off.

FINISHING
Using a flat seam, sew foot and back seam, reversing back seam above ribbing. Thread ribbon through yarn over (yo) holes and tie in a bow. Fold ankle section above ribbing to right side.

BOOTIES WITH RIBBED ANKLE
On Size 3 needles with MC, cast on 43 sts. Work as for Garter Stitch Booties to ***. Work 10 rows in st st (K1 row, P1 row).
Instep Shaping:
Next row: K37, K2tog, turn.
Next row: Sl 1, K9, K2tog, turn.
Next row: Sl 1, K9, K2tog, turn.
Rep last 2 rows until 45 sts rem (17 sts on each side of instep).
Next row: Sl 1, K9, K2tog, K16.
Next row: Purl – 44 sts.
Ankle:
Next row: K1, *yo, K2tog, rep from * to last st, K1.
Next row: Change to C. Purl, inc one st at each end – 46 sts.
Next row: K2, *P2, K2, rep from * to end.
Next row: P2, *K2, P2, rep from * to end.
Rep last 2 rows until ribbed section measures $3^1/_4$" from beg, ending with wrong side. End off.

FINISHING
Using a flat seam, sew foot and back seam, reversing back seam for $1^1/2$" at ankle edge. Thread ribbon through eyelet holes and tie in a bow. Fold half of ribbed section to right side.

❖
BABY'S PULLOVER

Average: For those with some experience in knitting and crochet.

To fit underarm	16"
Length	$9^1/2$"

MATERIALS
Fingering-weight 3 Ply yarn (50 g): 1 ball; 1 pair Size 3 and Size 2 knitting needles; Size C crochet hook; tapestry needle.

TENSION
On Size 3 needles in stockinette stitich (st st) – 8 sts = 1"; 11 rows = 1".

Directions:
BACK AND FRONT:
Using Size 2 needles, cast on 61 sts.
Row 1: K2, *P1, K1, rep from * to last st, K1.
Row 2: K1, *P1, K1, rep from * to end.
Rep Rows 1 and 2 until work measures $1^1/4$" from beg, ending with a 2nd row.
Change to Size 3 needles.

Fancy Fair Isle Booties

Work in st st (K1 row, P1 row), until work measures $6^1/2$" from beg, ending with a purl row.
Beg Pattern
Row 1: P2, *K3, yo, sl 1, K2tog, psso, yo, K3, P3, rep from * to last 11 sts, K3, yo, sl 1, K2tog, psso, yo, K3, P2.
Row 2: K2, *P9, K3, rep from * to last 11 sts, P9, K2.
Row 3: P2, *K1, K2tog, yo, K3, yo, sl 1, K1, psso, K1, P3, rep from * to last 11 sts, K1, K2tog, yo, K3, yo, sl 1, K1, psso, K1, P2.
Row 4: Rep Row 2.
Rep Rows 1 to 4, 3 times.
Neck Shaping:
Row 1: Work pat on 13 sts. Bind off. Work pat on 13 sts.
Cont on last 13 sts until work measures approx $9^1/2$" from beg, ending with a purl row. Bind off.
Join yarn to rem sts and work other side to correspond.

FINISHING

Using backstitch, join shoulder and side seams to beg of patt. With crochet hook, work 1 row single crochet evenly around neck having a number of sts divisible by 6. Next round: ch1 *1sc in first sc, sk 2sc, 5dc in next sc, skip sc, 2sc, rep from * to end, sl st in first ch1 at beg. Fasten off. Work same edging around armholes.

❖
FAIR ISLE BOOTIES

Average: For those with some experience in knitting.

To fit size 0-6 months

MATERIALS
Sport-weight yarn: 1 ball (50g) main color (MC), small quantities of 4 contrasting colors (A, B, C and D); 1 pair Size 5 knitting needles; ¼" wide ribbon; tapestry needle.

GAUGE
In stockinette stitch (st st) 26" sts = 4";

9 rows = 1".
Directions:
(Beg at sole)
With MC, cast on 31 sts.
Row 1: (Inc in next st, K13, inc in next st) twice, K1.
Rows 2, 4 and 6: Purl.
Row 3: (Inc in next st, K15, inc in next st) twice, K1.
Row 5: (Inc in next st, K17, inc in next st) twice, K1.
Row 7: (Inc in next st, K19, inc in next st) twice, K1.(47 sts).
Row 8: Knit.
Row 9: Purl.
Row 10: K3 (inc in next st, K4) 8 times, inc in next st, K3 – (56 sts).
With A, work 2 rows in st st.
Row 13: With B: K2* keeping yarn at back of work, Sl 1 purlwise, K2, rep from * to end.
Row 14: Purl.
With C, rep Rows 13 and 14 once.
With A, rep Rows 13 and 14 once.
Row 19: With MC: K3, (K2 tog, K4) 8 times, K2 tog, K3 – (47 sts).
Row 20: Knit.
Row 21: Purl.
Row 22: Knit.
Instep Shaping:
Row 23: K28, Sl 1 knitwise, K1, psso, turn.
Row 24: P10, P2 tog, turn.
Row 25: K10, Sl 1 knitwise, K1, psso, turn.
Rep Rows 24 and 25, 5 times, then Row 24 once.
Next row: K to end – (33 sts).
Proceed as follows:
Row 1: Purl.
Row 2: K1 * yo, K2 tog, rep from * to end.
Row 3: P1 * K1, P1, rep from * to end.
Row 4: K1 * P1, K1, rep from * to end.
Rep Rows 3 and 4 four times.
With A, knit 3 rows (to Row 15).
Row 16: K6 (inc in next st, K4) 4 times, inc in next st, K6.
Row 17: K2 *, keeping yarn at back of work, Sl 1 purlwise, K2, rep from * to end.
Row 18: Purl.
Row 19: With B K2 * keeping yarn at back of work, Sl 1 purlwise, K2, rep from * to end.
Row 20: Purl.
With C, rep Rows 19 and 20.
Change to A and K6, (K2 tog, K4) 4 times, K2 tog, K6 –(33 sts).
Knit next 2 rows.
Bind off knitwise.

FINISHING
Using backstitch, sew back seam, reversing seam half way. Using flat seam, join foot seam. Fold ankle sections over to right side. Thread ribbon through yarn over (yo) holes.

❖
KNITTED BALL

Average: For those with some experience in knitting and crochet.

Directions are given for a ball about 5½" in diameter.

MATERIALS:
Synthetic worsted-weight yarn (50 g): 1 ball of white (MC) and 1 ball each of purple (A), pale purple (B) and pink (C); 1 pair of Size 6 knitting needles; synthetic stuffing; tapestry needle.

GAUGE
On Size 9 needles with yarn doubled, working in garter stitch (K every row) – 15 sts = 4"; 6 rows = 1".
Note: Yarn is used doubled throughout.

First Section
On the Size 9 needles with double strand of MC, cast on 24 sts.
Row 1: Knit.
Row 2: Knit to last 4 sts, turn.
Row 3: Rep last row once.
Row 4: Knit to last 8 sts, turn.
Row 5: Rep last row once.
Row 6: Knit to end.
Row 7: Rep last row once.
Bind off loosely.
Work 2 more sections in MC, then 3 sections each in A, B and C.

FINISHING
Using backstitch, sew sections together as shown in photo. Draw thread through edge sts at bottom end and gather tightly. Fasten off securely. Stuff ball firmly, then draw thread through sts at other end. Gather and fasten off securely.

Knitted Ball

Dancing Dumpty and Knitted Ball

❖ DANCING DUMPTY ❖

Average: For those with some experience in knitting.

Height (excluding legs): about 7½".

MATERIALS
Bulky-weight yarn (50 g): 1 ball of white (MC) and 1 ball each of blue (A), pink (B) and yellow (C); 1 pair of Size 9 knitting needles; synthetic stuffing; 5½" of ⅝"-wide binding tape; scraps of red, black and pink felt; scrap of black yarn; 16½" length of gathered lace; 1¼" yards of ¼"-wide pink ribbon; 1 yard of ¼"-wide purple ribbon; tapestry needle, sewing thread and needle.

GAUGE
On Size 9 needles in stockinette stitch (st st) – 17 sts = 4"; 6 rows = 1".

Directions:
Body (beg at lower edge)
With MC cast on 6 sts.
Row 1: In st st, inc in each st to end – 12 sts.
Row 2: Purl.
Row 3: Rep Row 1 – 24 sts.
Work 3 rows in st st (K1 row, P1 row), beg with a purl row.

Row 7: Rep Row 1 – 48 sts.
Work 7 rows, inc one st each end of 1st row – 50 sts.
With A, work 6 rows.
With MC, work 6 rows.
Next row: K6, *K2tog, K10, rep from * to last 8 sts, K2tog, K6 – 46 sts.
Work even for 9 rows.
Next row: K5, *K2tog, K9, rep from * to last 8 sts, K2tog, K6 – 42 sts.
Work even for 3 rows.
Next row: K2, *K2tog, K2, rep from * to end – 32 sts.
Next row: Purl.
Next row: K2, *K2tog, K1, rep from * to end. – 22 sts.
Next row: Purl.
Next row: K1, (K2tog) 10 times, K1 – 12 sts.
Next row: Purl.
Next row: (K2tog) 6 times – 6 sts.
Break off yarn, pull end through rem sts, draw up and fasten off securely.

Arms (make 2 – beg at top)
With A, cast on 12 sts.
Work 4 rows in st st.
With MC, work 10 rows in st st.
Next row: (K2tog) 6 times – 6 sts.
Break off yarn, pull end through rem sts, draw up and fasten off securely.

Legs (make 2 – beg at top)
With MC, cast on 14 sts.
Work 18 rows in st st. With B, work 8 rows.
Next row: (K2tog) 7 times – 7 sts.
Break off yarn, pull end through rem sts, draw up and fasten off securely.

FINISHING
Using backstitch, join body seam, leaving an opening for stuffing, and drawing 6 "cast-on"sts together. Stuff firmly and stitch opening closed. Join arm and leg seams, leaving top edges open for stuffing. Stuff firmly and overcast stitch "cast-on"edges. Stitch arms to middle of body at sides, and stitch legs to body 2 rows up from last dec at beg. Cut eyes, nose and cheeks from felt and stitch in place. Embroider black yarn mouth using stem stitch. Stitch lace around body at first row of A.

To make hair sew a few loops of C yarn to forehead, using photo as guide. Cut remaining C into 20" lengths. Cut a 5½" length of tape and stitch center of lengths evenly along tape, leaving ⅜" of tape free at each end. Turn under ends of tape. Stitch hair (through tape) to head using photo as guide. Trim ends and tie into bunches using purple ribbon. Tie a purple bow to front. Tie pink ribbon around legs, using photo as a guide.

❖ VICTORIAN ROSE PILLOW ❖

Average: For those with some experience in cross stitch and sewing.

- [ ] **22-count white hardanger, 20"-square**
- [ ] **6-strand embroidery floss in colors indicated (use DMC colors or equivalent)**
- [ ] **firm cotton fabric, two pieces each 9 x 16$\frac{1}{2}$"**
- [ ] **3$\frac{1}{2}$ yards of 4"-wide lace**
- [ ] **16$\frac{1}{2}$"-square lightweight, white cotton**
- [ ] **16"-square pillow form**
- [ ] **12"-long zipper**
- [ ] **embroidery hoop**
- [ ] **sewing thread to match fabrics**

Directions:

1   Embroider rose motif and border in cross stitch following graph at right.

2   Pin embroidered panel on lightweight white cotton fabric. Baste together around edges.

3   Sew ends of Pillow back center seam ($\frac{3}{8}$" seam), leaving center 12" open for zipper. Attach zipper. Open zipper.

4   Gather lace to 64". Pin and baste lace around embroidered panel, right sides together, matching raw edges.

5   Pin pillow back and front together with right sides facing. Stitch around edges through all thicknesses. Turn to right side through zipper opening. Insert pillow form.

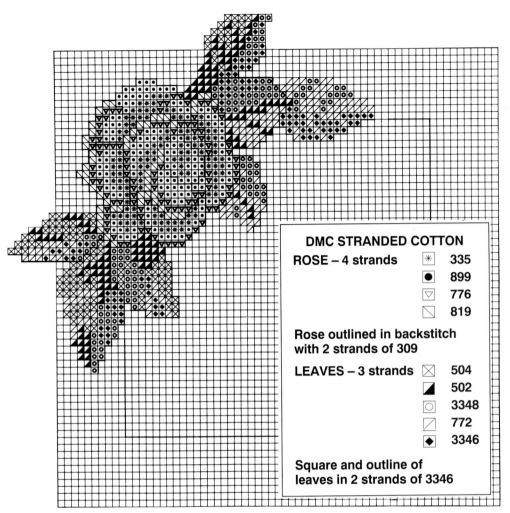

DMC STRANDED COTTON

ROSE – 4 strands

✳	335
●	899
▽	776
◻	819

Rose outlined in backstitch with 2 strands of 309

LEAVES – 3 strands

⊠	504
◨	502
◯	3348
◿	772
◆	3346

Square and outline of leaves in 2 strands of 3346

An embroidered pillow makes a popular raffle prize

Easy: Achievable by anyone.

37 inches long
- [ ] **strip of velvet 8¹⁄₂" x 45"**
- [ ] **embroidery floss in shades of pink and green**
- [ ] **strong ribbon or braid**
- [ ] **clean sand**
- [ ] **sewing thread to match fabric**
- [ ] **funnel**

Directions:

1   Embroider an oval of bullion roses in center of velvet and 10" from each end, following How to Embroider Bullion Roses, right.

2   Fold velvet with long sides even and right sides facing. Stitch long side, allowing ³⁄₈" seam. Turn.

3   Fold in 4" at one short end. Stitch and tie off very securely about 3¹⁄4" from end. Fill with sand, using a funnel. Shake frequently to settle sand. When tube is filled, fold in 4" at open end, stitch and tie off securely as before.

How To Embroider
BULLION ROSES

Bullion roses are stitched in gradient shades of embroidery floss, starting with darkest shade at center and working out to lightest shade. Stitch leaves in bullion knots or chain stitch in tones of green.

Bring needle up at A. Take a stitch from B to A; do not pull needle through (A to B equals the width of knot required). Twist thread several times around needle clockwise covering width of AB. Pull needle through easing twisted thread onto fabric. Reinsert needle at B. Build up bullion knots as shown below.

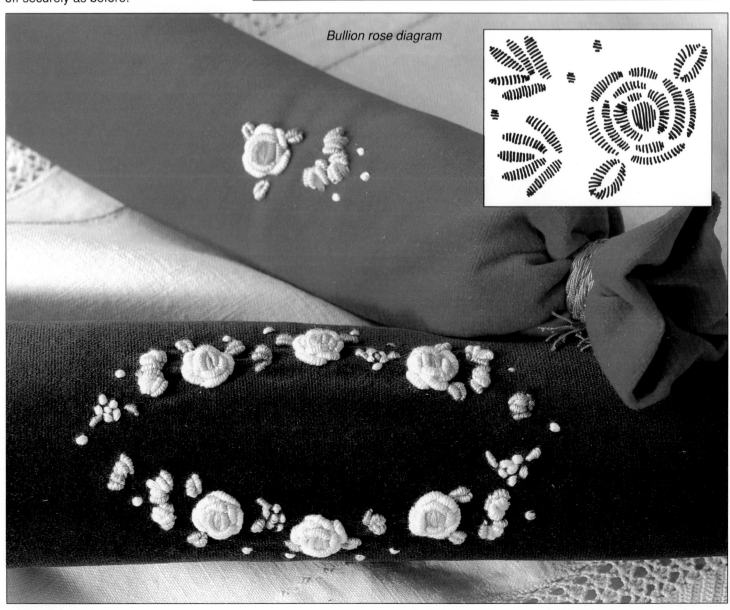

Bullion rose diagram

The ultimate draft stoppers embroidered with bullion roses

❖ HOT WATER BOTTLE ❖ COVER

Average: For those with some experience in sewing and embroidery.

- ☐ **two pieces open-weave, soft wool fabric, each 16" x 11¹/₂"**
- ☐ **24" of 1¹/₄"-wide cotton lace**
- ☐ **1 yard of ¹/₂"-wide satin ribbon**
- ☐ **crewel yarn**
- ☐ **sewing fabric to match fabric**

Directions:

1 Round off lower corners of both pieces of fabric. With crewel yarn, embroider flowers and leaves on front of one fabric piece, following diagram and using photo as a guide.

2 Pin fabric pieces together with right sides facing. Stitch both long sides and lower short end with ³/₈" seam, leaving 3¹/₄" open in sewn short end. Turn to right side.

3 Stitch around opening of sewn end, using blanket stitch and single strand of yarn, securing seam allowance as you go.

4 Stitch lace around open end. Thread ribbon through fabric, approximately 4" down from lace-trimmed edge and tie into bow. Or, make small buttonholes in fabric for ribbon.

Bullion roses embroidered on hot water bottle cover

EMBROIDERY TIP

Bullion roses are delightful, traditional embroidery motifs for the most feminine, personal and household items. Patience pays when stitching bullion roses, as the positioning of the petals determines the shape of your rose. Build up the stitches – placing some on top of others to give the rose depth and texture. Experts like to use five or six strands of floss when sewing, but experiment for yourself. The thicker the thread, the larger the rose, so for larger roses try working in wool yarn instead of embroidery floss. Remember, the first rose is by far the hardest to make!

Detail of hot water bottle cover embroidery

MOUSE IN A BALLOON

Average: For those with some experience in crafts.

BALLOON

- ☐ **6-inch polystyrene foam ball**
- ☐ **six 12 x 4-inch strips fabric in two or three coordinating prints**
- ☐ **three 20-inch lengths of 3/4-inch-wide insertion lace**
- ☐ **5 feet of 1/4-inch-wide satin ribbon**
- ☐ **1 yard 4 inches gathered lace**
- ☐ **small cane basket**
- ☐ **scrap fabric to line basket**
- ☐ **embroidery floss**
- ☐ **white glue**

MOUSE

- ☐ **squares white and scraps pink, blue and black felt**
- ☐ **polyester fibre for stuffing**
- ☐ **12 x 3 1/2-inch strip fabric for dress**
- ☐ **12-inch length broderie anglaise or wide lace for petticoat**
- ☐ **12 inches gathered lace**

EQUIPMENT

- ☐ **three large elastic rubber bands**
- ☐ **Stanley knife or sharp-pointed knife**
- ☐ **metal nail file**

Directions:

BALLOON

1 Divide foam ball into six equal segments using elastic rubber bands. It is best to lift and place bands into place rather than rolling them. When you are certain all segments are exactly equal, mark divisions with a fine pencil line.

2 With Stanley knife blade extended to about 4 3/4 inches and using a sawing action, cut along pencil lines, making sure they intersect at top and bottom of ball.

3 Cut six pieces of fabric to approximate size and shape of segments with 2 1/2-inch allowance all around. Pin each piece into place and, with a metal nail file, poke excess fabric carefully all the way into grooves already cut. Repeat until ball is covered.

4 Cut three lengths of insertion lace to go around ball through top and bottom points of intersection. Thread two 28-inch and one 30-inch length of ribbon into insertion lace, leaving approximately 8 1/2 inces of ribbon extending from one end of lace. These will attach to basket.

5 Measure 4 1/2 inches up every second line from intersection of lines on bottom of ball. Mark with a pencil. Beginning at one pencil mark, glue insertion lace with 28-inch ribbon down to bottom of ball and

around to pencil mark again. Do not overlap lace at join. Repeat for other 28-inch length. When glueing lace with 30-inch length of ribbon, draw out 2 inches of ribbon at top point of ball to form loop for hanging.

6 Mark 4 1/2 inches up from bottom along other three lines. These mark top of scallops of gathered lace. Draw in scalloped line with pencil to ensure it is even all around. Glue gathered lace along this line, making curves and points very pronounced and having lace join at one point. Glue bows to each point of scallops, covering join.

7 Glue free ends of ribbon, evenly spaced, around lip of small basket, taking care that basket hangs as straight as possible. It may be helpful to hold ribbons into place with pegs until glue dries.

8 Neaten raw edge of fabric scrap and handsew it inside basket. Decorate basket with lace and bows as shown.

MOUSE

1 Cut out one body piece. Fold double along foldline. Stitch seam, leaving base open. Trim seam and turn. Stuff firmly.

2 Run gathering thread around base. Pull up tightly and secure to close.

3 Embroider eyes and nose with satin stitch, taking threads from one to the other through head.

4 Glue pink inner ear to white outer ear with lower edges even. Fold ears in half at lower edge. Cut slits for ears in sides of head. Glue ears into slits.

5 Glue two foot pieces together for added stability. Glue on feet and tail.

6 To dress girl mouse, fold arms over double lengthways and glue to fix. Glue arms around body, approximately 1/2-inch below ears.

7 Press in 1/2-inch hem on top and lower edges of fabric strip for dress. Stitch lace around lower edge. Place top edge of petticoat under fold of top edge of dress. Gather top edge of dress and petticoat at same time. Cut slits for arms in dress and petticoat. Thread arms through. Shape hands. Tie bow on tail.

8 To dress boy mouse, glue on waistcoat with small amount of glue. Make arms as for girl and glue sleeves around them. Trim arms and shape hands. Fold and glue collar into place. Glue coat to mouse. Glue arms to mouse. Finish with bow tie, pearl stud and bow for tail.

Dainty lace and ribboned balloon with fashionably dressed mice

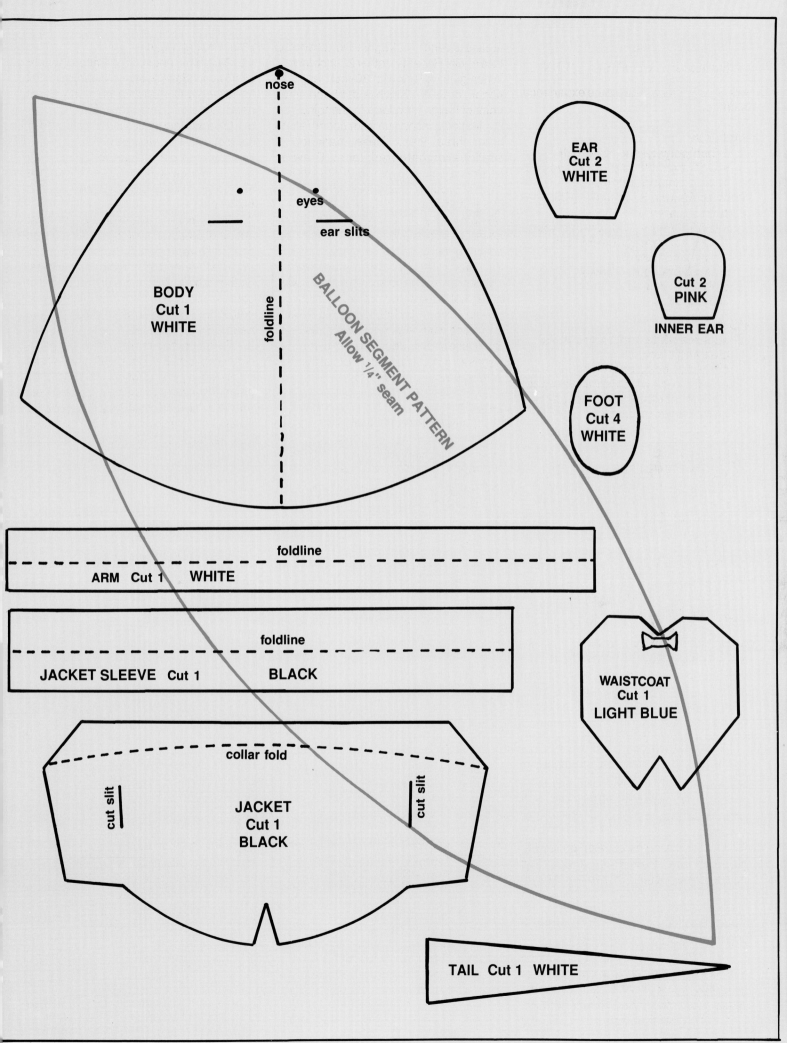

nose

eyes

ear slits

BODY
Cut 1
WHITE

foldline

BALLOON SEGMENT PATTERN
Allow ¼" seam

EAR
Cut 2
WHITE

Cut 2
PINK

INNER EAR

FOOT
Cut 4
WHITE

foldline

ARM   Cut 1   WHITE

foldline

JACKET SLEEVE   Cut 1   BLACK

WAISTCOAT
Cut 1
LIGHT BLUE

collar fold

cut slit

cut slit

JACKET
Cut 1
BLACK

TAIL   Cut 1   WHITE

MOUSE IN A BALLOON

Christmas corner

BREAD DOUGH ORNAMENTS

Make bread dough ornaments by combining 2 parts self-rising flour with 1 part each of salt and water. Knead thoroughly, adding food coloring if desired. Shape dough by rolling, coiling, braiding, cutting or squeezing through a garlic press, moistening each layer to attach.

Insert a paper clip at back for hanging. Bake at 225°F for 20 to 30 minutes or until ornaments are firm. Cool, then paint with clear polyurethane. *Note:* Baking time will vary according to size.

So many fairs are held before the holiday season – they are the perfect place to find unusual Christmas gifts, or decorations. Even if your fair is during the summer, stock a few Christmas items to keep folks in a merry mood.

Decorate the booth with our Christmas wreaths or use a small Christmas tree to show off our easy-to-make bread dough ornaments.

Create an attractive presentation by using our basket with mixed nuts as a centerpiece. Use as large a basket as possible and decorate as festively as you like with plenty of red and green ribbon. Or use several small baskets and arrange them around the booth.

For gift ideas, we have included deliciously scented sachets in a variety of shapes, sizes and fabrics which can be trimmed in any way you like. We even made some teddy bears (see page 52) in print fabrics especially for Christmas. People of all ages will love receiving their gifts in our Christmas stockings!

Don't forget how much everyone loves the "taste" of Christmas! Give your family and friends a good excuse to indulge with our delicious mini-puddings, chocolates and mixed nuts.

Try to have sprigs of fresh holly and mistletoe on hand to decorate packages. To make things even more festive, ask everyone who works in the booth to dress as one of Santa's elves!

❖ CHRISTMAS CHOCOLATES ❖

Makes about 25 squares or balls
- [ ] **1 cup mixed dried fruit**
- [ ] **3 tablespoons brandy**
- [ ] **14 squares (1 ounce each) unsweetened chocolate, melted**
- [ ] **1¹/₂ tablespoons vegetable shortening**
- [ ] **3 tablespoons chopped almonds**
- [ ] **flaked coconut (optional)**

1 Combine fruit and brandy in a non-metallic bowl; cover and set overnight.
2 Combine chocolate and shortening in a small, heavy saucepan. Melt over a low hear, stirring occasionally until smooth. Add to brandied fruit; stir in almonds. (If mixture is too wet, add some flaked coconut until desired consistency is obtained).
3 Spread mixture into 11 x 7 x 1¹/₂-inch baking pan. Refrigerate for several hours or until set. Cut into squares. If desired, refrigerate until partially set and shape into balls.
4 Wrap chocolates individually in cellophane. Tie with colored ribbon.

❖ BASKET WITH MIXED NUTS ❖

- [ ] **basket with lid**
- [ ] **2 yards of ³/₄"-wide plaid ribbon**
- [ ] **mixed nuts in shells**
- [ ] **white glue**
- [ ] **clear varnish**

Directions:
1 Glue lengths of plaid ribbon to basket lid, from one side to the other, crossing at center. Make loops of plaid ribbon and glue to center of lid. Glue lengths of ribbon to basket base beginning at lip and running down and around to other side.
2 Varnish a variety of nuts with clear varnish. Allow to dry. Glue nuts around and between ribbon loops on lid.
3 Fill basket with mixed nuts.

Far right: Christmas corner

1 To prepare Pudding: Break plum pudding into large chunks and place in the container of food processor or blender. Add rum or brandy, shortening and jam. Whirl until just combined. Form mixture into balls to fit cupcake liners. Refrigerate for several hours or until firm.

2 To prepare Frosting: Combine IOX (confectioners') sugar with milk and lemon juice in a small bowl. Beat until smooth. Drizzle frosting on top of puddings. Decorate with glacé fruits if you wish.

❖ CHRISTMAS STOCKINGS ❖

Average: For those with some experience in sewing.

Note: Exact fabric requirements depend on the print you choose:

- [ ] **Use 20" of 45"-wide vertically striped cotton fabric or 14" of 45"-wide all-over printed cotton or felt**
- [ ] **8" of 45"-wide contrasting cotton or felt**
- [ ] **14" lightweight synthetic batting**
- [ ] **gold braid, ribbon, lace, bells and holly for trimming**
- [ ] **tracing paper and pencil**
- [ ] **thread to match fabrics**
- [ ] **sewing machine bobbin (optional)**

Directions:

1 Trace and cut out pattern pieces following diagram on page 93. Cut two stocking shapes each from main fabric and batting. Cut two heels, two toes, two stocking tops from contrasting fabric or felt. For fabric stockings cut two top facings from contrasting fabric or felt. If you are using felt, cut scallops on inner edges of contrasting pieces by tracing around half shape of a sewing machine bobbin and cutting around outline.

2 Place batting pieces against wrong sides of stocking pieces; baste. Baste contrasting pieces in place, folding under any raw edges that will not be covered by decorative trims.

3 Stitch contrasting pieces and any decorative braid trims in place on stocking pieces. Scalloped felt pieces are stitched just inside scallops.

4 Place two stocking pieces together with right sides facing. Stitch. Clip seams. Turn and press. For felt stockings, stitch around top again, trimming felt close to stitching.

5 For fabric stockings, place top edges of facings together with right sides facing. Stitch short ends. Place facing around stocking top with right sides together. Stitch around top edge. Turn facing to inside. Press. Trim raw edge and hand-stitch inside stocking.

6 Stitch loop of braid or ribbon to top for hanging.

7 Stitch your choice of Christmas trims in place on stocking front, using photo (page 87) as a guide.

❖ CHRISTMAS WREATHS ❖

Easy: Achievable by anyone.

- [ ] **wreath form (available at florist or garden center)**
- [ ] **variety of trims, such as holly leaves and berries, seed pods, nuts, artificial fruit, flowers and ribbons**
- [ ] **floral wire**
- [ ] **spray paint, if desired**
- [ ] **hot melt glue gun, or white glue**

Directions:

1 If you wish, spray paint wreath form and allow to dry before decorating.

2 Plan your wreath arrangement before you begin to glue.

3 Prepare all trims – tie bows, spray paint nuts (if desired) and wire small items into bunches with floral wire.

4 Glue decorations in place on wreath form. Make a wire loop from doubled floral wire at center back for hanging wreath.

❖ REINDEER ❖

Average: For those with some experience in woodworking.

- [ ] **pieces of tree branches: about 1" thick and 2" long for head; 1³/₈" thick and 4" long for body; ⁵/₈" thick and 3" long for neck; ³/₈" thick and 1¹/₂" long for tail**
- [ ] **twigs for antlers**
- [ ] **scraps leather or vinyl**
- [ ] **four ³/₈"-diameter dowels, each 4" long**

Beautiful Christmas decorations

- [ ] **white paper and black felt-tip pen**
- [ ] **holly, berries, gold cord and other Christmas trims**
- [ ] **white glue, or hot-melt glue gun**
- [ ] **drill with ³/₈-inch bit**

Directions:

1 Drill small holes for twig antlers on top of head piece. Glue antlers in place.

2 Cut out ear shapes from leather or vinyl scraps. Glue ears in place on side of head.

3 Drill holes for dowel legs in body. Position legs so that reindeer stands securely. Glue legs in place. Glue head to neck. Glue neck to body. Glue on tail at an angle.

6 Cut out eyes from white paper, draw in pupils with felt-tip pen. Glue on eyes.

7 Trim with Christmas trims. Glue on cord at top of head for hanging.

❖ MINI CHRISTMAS ❖ PUDDINGS

Makes 6 mini puddings

PUDDING

- [ ] **1 can (14 ounces) plum pudding**
- [ ] **2 tablespoons rum or brandy**
- [ ] **1¹/₂ tablespoons vegetable shortening, melted**
- [ ] **2 tablespoons raspberry jam**
- [ ] **cupcake liners**

FROSTING

- [ ] **1¹/₄ cups IOX (confectioners') sugar**
- [ ] **1 to 2 tablespoons milk**
- [ ] **1 to 2 teaspoons lemon juice**
- [ ] **glacé fruits (optional)**

❖ RICH FRUIT CAKES

Makes 2 cakes

- [ ] **2 pounds mixed fruit**
- [ ] **1¹/₂ cups dates, chopped**
- [ ] **¹/₂ cup (1 stick) butter**
- [ ] **³/₄ cup firmly packed brown sugar**
- [ ] **1 teaspoon ground cinnamon**
- [ ] **¹/₂ cup water**
- [ ] **¹/₂ cup brandy**
- [ ] **2 eggs, lightly beaten**
- [ ] **1 cup all-purpose flour**
- [ ] **1 cup self-rising flour**
- [ ] **glacé cherries for decoration**
- [ ] **whole blanched almonds for decoration**

1   Preheat the oven to moderate (325°). Grease and line two 9 x 5 x 3-inch loaf pans.

2   Place mixed fruit, dates, butter, sugar, cinnamon and water in a large saucepan and cook over a medium heat, stirring, until butter melts. Bring to a boil, then reduce heat and simmer, uncovered, for 3 minutes. Remove pan from heat and cool to room temperature.

3   Stir brandy and eggs into fruit mixture. Sift together all-purpose flour and self-rising flour, add to fruit mixture and mix well to combine. Divide batter between the two loaf pans and bake in preheated moderate oven (325°) for 1¹/₄-1¹/₂ hours or until a wooden pick inserted in the center comes out clean. Cool for 10 minutes in the pans, then turn onto clean tea towels to cool completely.

❖ SHORTBREAD JEWELS

Makes 24 squares

- [ ] **1 cup (2 sticks) butter, cut into small pieces**
- [ ] **²/₃ cup superfine sugar**
- [ ] **¹/₂ cup ground rice**
- [ ] **3 cups all-purpose flour, sifted**
- [ ] **¹/₂ cup red glacé cherries**
- [ ] **¹/₂ cup green glacé cherries**
- [ ] **1 cup blanched almonds**

1   Preheat the oven to moderate (325°). Lightly grease a 7 x 11 x 1¹/₂-inch shallow cake pan.

2   Place butter and sugar in a food processor and process to combine. With machine running, slowly add ground rice and flour and continue processing until mixture forms a ball. Turn dough onto a lightly floured surface and knead briefly.

3   Press dough into the prepared cake pan and using the tip of a sharp knife mark lightly into 2-inch squares. Decorate each square with red and green glacé cherries and almonds.

4   Bake in preheated moderate oven (325°) for 40 minutes, or until shortbread is a pale straw color. Cool in pan placed on a wire rack, then cut into squares.

❖ CHRISTMAS TREE COOKIES

Makes about 45 cookies

- [ ] **3 cups all-purpose flour, sifted**
- [ ] **2 teaspoons baking powder**
- [ ] **2 teaspoons ground cinnamon**
- [ ] **1 teaspoon pumpkin pie spice**
- [ ] **1 teaspoon ground ginger**
- [ ] **¹/₄ teaspoon salt**
- [ ] **1 cup (2 sticks) butter or margarine, softened**
- [ ] **1¹/₂ cups packed brown sugar**
- [ ] **¹/₄ cup brandy, rum or orange juice**
- [ ] **1 egg white, lightly beaten**
- [ ] **golden raisins, raisins, almonds and glacé cherries to decorate**

1   Preheat the oven to moderate (350°). Lightly grease cookie sheets.

2   Sift together flour, baking powder, cinnamon, pumpkin pie spice, ginger and salt into a bowl and set aside. Beat butter until creamy, continue beating while gradually adding sugar. Mix in rum, brandy or orange juice, then add flour mixture and continuing mixing until well combined and a soft dough forms. Wrap dough in plastic food wrap and chill for 30 minutes.

3   Turn out dough onto a lightly floured surface and roll out to ¹/₄-inch thick. Cut dough into shapes using decorative cookie cutters such as bells, stars, hearts and gingerbread men.

4   Place cookies on cookie sheets and brush with egg white. Using a metal skewer mark patterns on each cookie and decorate with raisins, cherries and almonds. Make a hole in the top of each cookie for threading ribbon through and bake in preheated moderate oven (350°) for 15 minutes or until firm to the touch. Cool on wire racks. Thread ribbon through holes in cookies, wrap in cellophane and store in an airtight container.

Rich Fruit Cakes

EASY CHRISTMAS PUDDING

Wrap Christmas Puddings in cellophane and attach a label with reheating instructions. This pudding will take 4-5 minutes to reheat in the microwave.

Serves 6

- ☐ ¹/₂ cup (1 stick) butter
- ☐ ¹/₂ cup firmly packed brown sugar
- ☐ 2 eggs
- ☐ 1¹/₂ cups self-rising flour
- ☐ 1 teaspoon pumpkin pie spice
- ☐ pinch salt
- ☐ 1¹/₄ cup dried mixed fruit
- ☐ ¹/₂ cup dried dates, chopped
- ☐ ¹/₄ cup glacé cherries, halved
- ☐ ¹/₃ cup sherry or orange juice

1   Place butter and sugar in a bowl and beat until light and fluffy. Beat in eggs one at a time, beating well after each addition.
2   Sift flour, pumpkin pie spice and salt together and stir into butter mixture.
3   Add mixed fruit, dates, cherries and sherry or orange juice and mix well to combine.
4   Spoon batter into a greased 4-cup pudding basin, cover with a large piece of greased aluminum foil. If basin has a lid, place the lid over the foil and bring the surplus foil up over it. If the basin has no lid, tie the foil securely in position, using string. Place basin on an upturned saucer in a large saucepan with enough boiling water to come half way up the sides of the basin and steam for 2 hours. Add more water as necessary during cooking. On completion of cooking remove basin from pan and set aside to cool to room temperature.

CHRISTMAS MINCE PIES

The flavor of the fruit mince develops and grows richer with time, so try to store for at least a week before making pies. Rather than making the pies you might like to sell jars of fruit mince and include the instructions for making the pies.

Makes 12 pies

FRUIT MINCE
- ☐ ³/₄ cup currants
- ☐ ³/₄ cup golden seedless raisins
- ☐ ³/₄ cup raisins, chopped
- ☐ ³/₄ cup mixed candied citrus peel
- ☐ 1 cup suet, finely grated
- ☐ ³/₄ cup almonds, finely chopped
- ☐ 1 large Granny Smith apple, peeled and grated
- ☐ ¹/₄ cup lemon juice
- ☐ ¹/₄ cup orange juice
- ☐ 2 teaspoons finely grated lemon rind
- ☐ 2 teaspoons finely grated orange rind
- ☐ 1 cup canned crushed pineapple, drained
- ☐ ¹/₂ cup firmly packed brown sugar
- ☐ 1 teaspoon pumpkin pie spice
- ☐ ¹/₃ cup brandy or sherry

PASTRY
- ☐ ¹/₂ cup (1 stick) butter
- ☐ ¹/₂ cup superfine sugar
- ☐ 1 egg
- ☐ 1 cup self-rising flour
- ☐ 1 cup all-purpose flour
- ☐ 1 egg white, lightly beaten
- ☐ sifted IOX (confectioners') sugar to finish

1   To make mince, place currants, golden seedless raisins, raisins, citrus peel, suet, almonds, apple, lemon juice, orange juice, lemon rind, orange rind, pineapple, brown sugar, pumpkin pie spice and brandy or sherry in a large bowl and mix well to combine. Spoon mince into jars, seal and store in the refrigerator until required.
2   Preheat the oven to moderate (350°). Grease 12 regular muffin-pan cups.
3   To make pastry, place butter and sugar in a bowl and beat until light and fluffy. Beat in egg. Sift together self-rising flour and flour and fold into butter mixture. Turn dough onto a lightly floured surface and knead briefly. Wrap in plastic wrap and chill for 1 hour.

4   Divide dough into two portions and roll out one portion to ¹/₄-inch thick. Using a 3-inch cutter, cut out 12 pastry rounds and place in muffin pans. Spoon fruit mince into shells.
5   Roll out remaining pastry and using a star-shaped or round cutter, cut out 12 lids and place on top of filling. Brush with egg white and bake in the preheated moderate oven (350°) for 25 minutes, or until pastry is golden. Stand pies in pans for 1 minute before removing to wire racks to cool.

WHITE CHRISTMAS

Wrap bars of White Christmas individually in cellophane and tie each end with a bright ribbon. Pack into a pretty box or tin or arrange in a small basket.

Makes 20 bars

- ☐ 1 cup flaked coconut
- ☐ 1 cup full-cream milk powder
- ☐ 1 cup IOX (confectioners') sugar, sifted
- ☐ ¹/₄ cup raisins, chopped
- ☐ ¹/₄ cup candied pineapple, chopped
- ☐ ¹/₄ cup mixed candied citurs peel
- ☐ 2 cups unsweetened puffed rice cereal
- ☐ 1 cup solid vegetable shortening, melted
- ☐ 1 teaspoon vanilla extract

1   Place coconut, milk powder, IOX (confectioners') sugar, raisins, pineapple, citrus peel and rice cereal in a bowl and mix to combine. Stir in vegetable shortening and vanilla and mix well.
2   Press mixture into a lightly greased shallow 7 x 11 x 1¹/₂-inch cake pan, smooth top and chill until firm. Cut into bars.

Easy Christmas Pudding

HEAVEN SCENT

Wonderful scented sachets in a variety of shapes and sizes are always popular bazaar items. Make them in any lightweight fabric and trim with narrow or wide ribbon bows and silk, artificial or dried flowers. Sachets may be filled with potpourri, lavender, scented wax chips or cedar shavings. Make some pine and cinnamon-scented sachets just for the holidays. For a very simple and inexpensive filling, moisten a cotton ball with your choice of perfumed oil and wrap it in synthetic stuffing.

❖ CIRCULAR SCENTED ❖ BUNDLES

Easy: Achievable by anyone.

- [ ] **scraps of pretty cotton print fabric, voile, lace or mesh in desired size**
- [ ] **lace and ribbon trims**
- [ ] **small wooden curtain ring**
- [ ] **$1/8$"- wide satin ribbon**
- [ ] **artificial or dried flowers**
- [ ] **your choice of fillings: cedar shavings for moth protection, lavender or potpourri for sweet smells, or synthetic stuffing, enclosing a cotton ball saturated with perfumed oil**
- [ ] **thread to match fabric**
- [ ] **pinking shears (optional)**

Directions:
1   Cut a circle of fabric at least 10 inches in diameter. Finish edges with pinking shears, zigzag stitch or hem. Or stitch lace around edge.
2   Stitch a gathering row $3/4$" from edge. Make ruffle narrower or wider by stitching this row closer to or farther from edge. Draw up gathering threads slightly.
3   Fill bundle, and close by pulling up gathering threads tightly. Tuck dried flowers into bundle if desired. Tie threads to secure.
4   Tie ribbon bows around gathering and tuck flowers into bow.
5   Using buttonhole stitch, weave $1/8$"-wide ribbon around curtain ring to cover. Stitch bundles to hanging ring through ribbon.

Lovely scented sachets trimmed with bows and flowers

❖ SACHETS ❖

Easy: Achievable by anyone.

- [ ] **scraps of fabric or lace 6" x 7"**
- [ ] **tulle scraps in same size**
- [ ] **lace and ribbon**
- [ ] **potpourri**
- [ ] **thread to match fabric**
- [ ] **embroidery floss (optional)**

Directions:
If you plan to embroider sachet, do it before you sew. Embroider motif of your choice or see How To Embroider Bullion Roses (page 82).
1   Place fabric or lace and tulle lining together and fold in half, with right sides together, to form sachets 3 1/2"-wide.
2   Stitch both sides. Turn and press.
3   If fabric is unfinished at top edge, turn in $1/4$" and then another $3/4$". Stitch. Stitch narrow lace around top edge of sachet or wider lace around throat to decorate.
4   Fill with potpourri to about 2" from top edge. Tie ribbon around throat to secure.

❖ TALCUM-FILLED ❖ RIBBONS

Easy: Achievable by anyone.

- [ ] **20" lengths of $1 1/2$"-wide patterned lace or picot-edge satin ribbon**
- [ ] **$1/8$"-wide ribbon**
- [ ] **talcum powder (purchased, or made yourself following directions below)**
- [ ] **thread to match ribbon**

Directions:
1   To make talcum powder, combine in a bowl 3 parts cornstarch to 1 part orris root powder to two teaspoons of your favorite floral-scented oil. Mix well and store in an airtight jar for about a month, mixing occasionally.
2   Fold 1 1/2" ribbon in half with wrong sides facing. Stitch sides.
3   Fold in 1 1/2" ends at top. Fill ribbon with talcum powder. Tie $1/8$"-wide bow around top to secure.

❖ DOILY SACHETS ❖

Easy: Achievable by anyone.

- [ ] **small cotton lace doily**
- [ ] **tulle**
- [ ] **narrow ribbon**
- [ ] **potpourri, lavender or cedar shavings**
- [ ] **thread to match doily**

Directions:
1   Baste doily and tulle together.
2   Stitch around inner circle of doily, forming a pocket for potpourri and leaving a small opening for stuffing. Trim away excess tulle. Fill with potpourri, lavender or cedar shavings. Close opening by hand. If doily center is a very open weave, line it with an extra layer of tulle and back it with tulle. Fill between two layers of tulle.
3   Trim with bows and ribbons. Attach a ribbon loop for hanging sachet, if desired.

❖ BONBONS ❖

Easy: Achievable by anyone.

- [ ] **7" of double-edged scalloped lace about 8" wide**
- [ ] **tulle for lining in same size**
- [ ] **ribbon**
- [ ] **potpourri or desired filling**
- [ ] **thread to match lace**

Directions:
1   Place lace and tulle lining together and stitch raw edges together to form a 3 1/8" x 8" tube. Turn.
2   Tie a ribbon bow around one scalloped end.
3   Fill tube with potpourri and tie bow around other end.

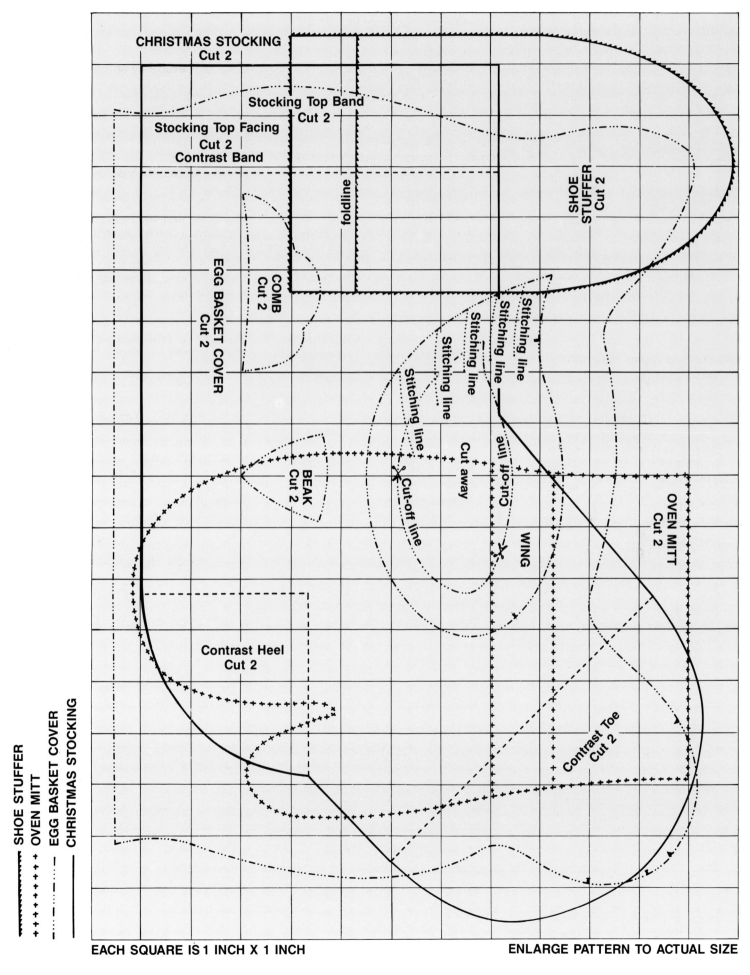

CHRISTMAS STOCKING
Cut 2

Stocking Top Band
Cut 2

Stocking Top Facing
Cut 2
Contrast Band

foldline

SHOE
STUFFER
Cut 2

EGG BASKET COVER
Cut 2

COMB
Cut 2

Stitching line

Stitching line

Stitching line

Stitching line

Cut away

Cut-off line

BEAK
Cut 2

Cut-off line

WING

OVEN MITT
Cut 2

Contrast Heel
Cut 2

Contrast Toe
Cut 2

SHOE STUFFER
OVEN MITT
EGG BASKET COVER
CHRISTMAS STOCKING

EACH SQUARE IS 1 INCH X 1 INCH

ENLARGE PATTERN TO ACTUAL SIZE

Craft Index

Appliquéd towels 68
Baby's clothes
   bootees 78
   cardigan and
      cap 76
   Fair Isle bootees 79
   pullover 78
Ball, knitted 79
Bangle, hairband and comb 61
Baskets
   herb 49
   with mixed nuts 86
Bath oils 51
Bed socks 74
Bonbons, scented 92
Bootees 78
   Fair Isle 79
Bread dough ornaments 86
Bullion roses 82
Cap, baby's 76
Christmas stockings 88
Christmas decorations
   reindeer 88
   wreaths 88
Coat hanger
   cover 62, 74
   gathered 62
   with gathered top 62
Combs, hairband and
   bangles 61
Dancing dumpty 80
Doily sachets 92
Draft stoppers 82
Dried herbs 51
Egg basket cover 66
Flower pots 56
Flower press 56
Hair ribbon holder 62
Hairband, bangles and
   combs 61
Hat, sun 56

Herbs
   baskets 49
   dried 51
   vinegars 51
Hot water bottle cover 83
Knitted ball 79
Mouse 64
   in a balloon 84
Mushroom bag 56
Nut basket 86
Oven mitt 67
Picture frames, fabric-
   covered 60
Pillow
   Victorian rose 81
   teddy bear 56
Pincushion 60
   pine cone 61
Pine cone pincushion 61
Place mats
   with contrasting centres 68
   with shaped corners 69
Plants, potted 48
Pot holder 67
Potpourri 50
Pots, flower 56
Potted plants 48
Pullover, baby's 78
Reindeer 88
Ribbons
   holder 62
   roses 60
   talcum-filled 92
Sachets, scented 92
Scented sachets 92
Scented shoe stuffers 63
Sewing kit 66
Shoe stuffers, scented 63
Shower cap 67
Stencilling 56
Stockings, Christmas 88

Sun hat 56
Table napkin
   with contrasting border 69
   with embroidered trim 69
Talcum-filled ribbons 92
Tea cosy 74
Teddy bear 63
   pillow 56
Toilet paper holder 68
Toiletry bag 67
Towels, appliquéd 68
Toys
   dancing dumpty 80
   knitted ball 79
   mouse 64
   mouse in a balloon 84
   teddy bear 63
Victorian rose 81
Vinegars, herb 51
Wreaths, Christmas 88

Recipe Index

Almond
  Cookies 21
  Pecan Brittle 31
  Truffles 30
Apples
  Cake 13
  Candy 26
  Chutney 38
Apricots
  Balls 30
  Brandied 37
  Jam 39
Banana Cake 13
Bars
  Caramel Crunch 32
  Chocolate Almond
    Squares 34
  Date 24
  Fruity Cereal Squares 24
  Ginger Crunch 24
  Honey Malt 21
  Lemon and Lime 23
  Lemon and Pistachio Nut
    Bars 24
  Muesli 21
Best Ever Chocolate Cake 10
Blueberry and Apple
  Muffins 43
Brandied Apricots 37
Bread and Butter Cucumbers 37
Bun, Chelsea 45
Butter Cake 12
Butterscotch 32
Cake
  see also Loaf
  Apple 13
  Banana 13
  Best Ever Chocolate 10
  Butter 12
  Coconut 13
  Coffee 13
  Orange 13

Quick Mix Fruit 16
  Rich Fruit 89
Candy Apples 26
Caramel Crunch 32
Caramels
  Creamy 31
  Fruit and Nut 32
  Sesame 34
Chelsea Bun 45
Chewy Jewels 30
Chicken Liver Pâté 41
Chocolate
  Almond Squares 34
  Cake 10
  Chip Cookies 21
  Eclairs 23
  Frosting 15, 17
  Mocha Icing 10
Chocolates
  Almond Fudge Squares 32
  Cashew Toffee 34
  Christmas 86
  Crackles 34
  Nut Creams 29
  Nut Wreaths 35
  Rum Truffles 30
Christmas Chocolates 86
Christmas Mince Pies 91
Christmas Puddings 88, 91
Christmas Tree Cookies 89
Chutney
  Spicy Apple 38
  Tomato Relish 38
Cinnamon Cookies 23
Coconut
  Cake 13
  Covered Cakes 28
  Haystacks 28
Coconut Covered Cakes 17
Coffee
  Cake 13
  Frosting 15

Confectionery see Sweets
Cookies
  see also Bars
  Almond Cookies 21
  Chocolate Chip Cookies 21
  Christmas Tree Cookies 89
  Cinnamon 23
  Ginger Snaps 23
  Gingerbread Family 18
  Hazelnut Fingers 21
  Orange Shortbread 21
  Shortbread Creams 23
  Shortbread Jewels 89
  Tuiles 32
Cornflake Crunchies 32
Creamy Caramels 31
Cucumbers, Bread and
  Butter 37
Date Bars 24
Date Scones 42
Eclairs, Chocolate 23
Fig Jam 39
Frosting
  Chocolate 15, 17
  Chocolate Mocha 10
  Coffee 15
  Lemon Cream Cheese 15
  Mocha 21
  Orange Cream 15
  Royal 18
Fruit and Nut Caramels 32
Fruit and Nut Rolls 43
Fruit Cake, Quick Mix 16
Fruit Cakes, Rich 89
Fruity Cereal Squares 24
Ginger Crunch 24
Ginger Snaps 23
Gingerbread Family 18
Hazelnut Fingers 21
Honey Malt Bars 21
Honeycomb 30
Horseradish Mustard 39

Jam
    Apricot 39
    Fig 39
    Plum 38
    Strawberry 43
    Three Fruit Marmalade 39
Lemon
    Butter 39
    Cream Cheese Frosting 15
    and Lime Bars 23
    and Pistachio Nut Bars 24
Loaf
    Fruit and Nut Rolls 43
    Pecan Fruit 45
    Zucchini and Walnut 16
Marmalade, Three Fruit 39
Marshmallows, Toasted 29
Mince Pies 91
Mini Raisin Pancakes 45
Mocha Frosting 21
Muesli Bars 21
Muffins, Blueberry and
    Apple 43
Mustard, Horseradish 39
Onions, Pickled 36
Orange
    Cake 13
    Cream Frosting 15
    Shortbread 21
Pâté
    Chicken Liver 41
    Salmon 41
Pancakes, Mini Raisin 45
Pecan Fruit Loaf 45
Pickled Onions 36
Pies, Pork 41
Plum Jam 38
Pork Pies 41
Puddings, Christmas 88, 91
Quick Mix Fruit Cake 16
Raisin Pancakes, Mini 45
Raisin Scones 42
Relish *see* Chutney
Rocky Road 29
Royal Icing 18

Rum Balls 31
Salmon Pâté 41
Scones 42
Sesame Caramels 34
Shortbread
    Creams 23
    Jewels 89
    Orange 21
Strawberry Jam 43
Sweets
    see also Caramels;
        Chocolates
    Almond-Pecan Brittle 31
    Almond Truffles 30
    Apricot Balls 31
    Butterscotch 32
    Coconut Haystacks 28
    Cornflake Crunchies 32
    Creamy Caramels 31
    Honeycomb 30
    Rocky Road 29
    Rum Balls 31
    Toasted Marshmallows 29
    Walnut Crunchies 35
    White Christmas 91
Three Fruit Marmalade 39
Toasted Marshmallows 29
Tomato Relish 38
Truffles
    Almond 30
Tuiles 32
Walnut Crunchies 35
White Christmas 91
Zucchini and Walnut Loaf 16